The First Boxers

By James LaFond
Illustrated by Joseph Bellofatto

The First Boxers: A Fighter's View of Prize-Fighting from Gilgamesh to Goliath

"LaFond writes like an angel with a razor—he is careful and precise, but with a light touch and an accurate eye for what will entertain and delight as well as inform and enlighten."

-Professor David Carl, Saint John's College at Santa Fe

Books by James LaFond

Nonfiction

The Fighting Edge, 2000
The Logic of Steel, 2001
The First Boxers, 2011
The Gods of Boxing, 2011
All Power Fighting, 2011
When You're Food, 2011
The Lesser Angles of Our Nature, 2012
The Logic of Force, 2012
The Greatest Boxer, 2012
Take Me to Your Breeder, 2014
The Streets Have Eyes, 2014
Panhandler Nation, 2014
The Ghetto Grocer, 2014
American Fist, 2014
Don't Get Boned, 2014
Alienation Nation, 2014
In The Chinks of The Machine, 2014
How the Ghetto Got My Soul, 2014
Saving the World Sucks, 2014
Taboo You, 2014
The Fighting Life, 2014
Narco Night Train, 2014
Into the Mountains of Madness, 2014

Fiction

Astride the Chariot of Night, 2014
Sacrifix, 2014
Rise, 2014
Motherworld, 2014
Planet Buzzkill, 2014
Fruit of The Deceiver, 2014
Forty Hands of Night, 2014
Black and Pale, 2014
Daughters of Moros, 2014
Fat Girl, 2014
Hurt Stoker, 2014
Poet, 2014
Triumph, 2015
Winter, 2015
The Spiral Case, 2015
Hemavore, with Dominick Mattero, 2015
Yusuf of the Dusk, 2015
Mantid, 2015
RetroGenesis: Day 1, with Erique Watson, 2015

Sunset Saga Novels
Big Water Blood Song, 2011
Ghosts of the Sunset World, 2011
Beyond the Ember Star, 2012
Comes the Six Winter Night, 2012
Thunder-Boy, 2012
The World is Our Widow, 2013
Behind the Sunset Veil, 2013
Den of The Ender, 2013
God's Picture Maker, 2014
Out of Time, 2015
Seven Moons Deep, 2015

Originally published as an html e-book in 2011

Prepared for publication by Jamie King in arrangement with Punch Buggy Books editingbyjamie@gmail.com

Research Assistance: Erika Cooper, Baltimore County Public Library

Critical Reading: Professor David Carl of Saint John's College at Santa Fe; Jay Harding EDS. University of Iowa, Kenpo & kali instructor; Doctor David Lumsden, MMA coach.

Instruction: "Reds" Foley; Ed Jones; "Irish" Johnny Coiley; Arturo Gabriel; Frank Gilbert; Jimmy Hines; Dan Funk

This is the first of four volumes that comprise *The Broken Dance: A Fighter's View of Boxing and Prize-fighting from Pre-history to the Fall of Rome.*

For Jimmy Hines, who won his first 100 fights before giving up the ring for the Korean battlefield.

Contents

The Illustrator

Joseph Bellofatto Junior's paintings and illustrations have been featured on the covers and interiors of *Absolute Magnitude* and *Gateways Magazine*, and books by *Quite Vision Publishing*. He won an honorable mention in the L. Ron Hubbard *Writers Artist of the Future* contest. He lives with his wife, children and dogs in suburban Maryland.

The Author

James LaFond lives and works in the "once great medieval city" of Baltimore Maryland. He has fought 20 submission boxing bouts according to LPR, Gypsy and Greek rules, for 7 wins, 4 losses and 9 draws. James can be reached directly at www.jameslafond.com

Introduction

"Do not rely on your strength alone,
but be watchful, be wary, make every blow count."
-Gilgamesh

James LaFond has achieved a rare accomplishment in his most recent book, *The Broken Dance*. Reaching back into the farthest reaches of man's history, he follows the elusive thread of man's efforts to formalize his basic instinct towards violence. From Gilgamesh to Mike Tyson, LaFond's work unearths and explores the facts of formal combat and uses them as a point of departure for more far-ranging questions about the very nature of man's relationship to violence. Marshalling an impressive body of ancient literature, art, and history, LaFond argues that it was through our attempts to ritualize our inevitably violent tendencies towards each other and the world that civilization itself began to take shape.

-Professor David Carl, Saint John's College at Santa Fe

The King of Sports

Wrestling is the only sport known to have been practiced by prehistoric man. Wrestling was the first sport and the first unarmed martial art; the father of sports and prize-fighting.

The second sport was boxing; the king of sports. Boxing is the most brutal combat sport. As a practice, ritualized fist-fighting in the ancient Western World, evolved as a sacral act among the Indo-European war-chiefs who conquered the Near East, Egypt and Eastern Europe between 2000 and 1000 B.C. Nowhere does boxing emerge in the absence of the war-chariot: weapon of the duelist; tool of the prehistoric blitzkrieg; and, viewed quite literally, as the vehicle of the gods. The practice of boxing was developed as part of a social and martial support system for military elites descended from shepherds and cattle-men who ruled vast conquered populations of farmers.

This was a world where killing enemies was a sacred act sanctioned by the Sky-god; where slaughtering and enslaving the weak worshippers of the Earth Mother, who farmed the river valleys, was all in a day's work; where the head-of-state was expected to duel to the death; where even God had bloody hands. In the ancient world one cannot separate boxing from religion or war, or from other types of prize-fighting such as wrestling and stick-fighting. We are about to visit a world where a man's identity as a warrior—as an efficient killer of men and owner of horses and slaves—was all that separated him from the slave toiling in the mud beneath the burning sky that literally sanctioned his misery.

Welcome to the brutal world of the First Boxers.

Chapter 1
In Search of the First Boxers

In 1998 I began research on a comprehensive study of boxing methods and their social context. My initial reading of 132 books on boxing led me to believe that there was very limited extant information on boxing in ancient times. This was to be a comprehensive study of boxing methods, with an overview of the settings they were practiced in, from prehistory to the present. I gained access to some rare book collections and spent 18 months completing my initial reading of 1,152 books.

As the reading progressed I consulted with my editor, John Ford, who advised me to keep "cutting the head off" of the book as the roots grew deeper, so that we would have a manageable piece that could be published. Twenty-seven times I "cut the head off", until finally paring it back to a 700 page document that ended in 323 B.C. with the death of Alexander. Even this manuscript, single-spaced as it was, was too large for practical publication. The glossary on Greek martial terminology ran to 62 pages.

I have taken that manuscript and re-written it into three volumes: *The First Boxers: A Fighter's View of Prize-Fighting from Gilgamesh to Goliath*, which had been the first portion of the book; *The Gods of Boxing: A Fighter's View of Boxing from*

Achilles to Alexander, developed from the two largest chapters of the book; and *All-Power-Fighting: A Fighter's View of Mixed Martial Arts from Achilles to Alexander*. I do intend to transform the notes and outline for the remainder of the ancient period into a fourth volume: *The Boxer Dread: A Fighter's View of Boxing and Mixed Martial Arts from Alexander to the Fall of Rome.*

There may be some deductions on the origin of boxing that the reader may feel rest on mere shreds of evidence. In some cases this is true. My theory on the social context of Cretan boxing is just that, a theory. However, as to the origins of boxing, much of the supporting evidence comes from the Greek period, and will be presented in *The Gods of Boxing*; and, particularly where the question of the chariot is concerned, in *All-Power-Thing*. For an in-depth discussion of my utilization of the literary source material, one must also wait for the second volume, the last chapter of which is a bibliophile's wet dream.

For the modern fighter or coach the subjects of our study must seem dead and distant indeed, rarely with even a name to proclaim who these fighters once were. We walk though, in their very shadow, both literally and figuratively. These men were made of the same material as we; felt pain, new exhaustion, savored victory, and tasted defeat. It can only be guessed if they had the same hopes and dreams that we possess. But they walked on this very same earth, trained under the same uncaring sun, and fought before spectators that were equally as in capable of understanding them, as the people who have watched us beat one another during our journey. I, for one, think they would be honored to know that some knucklehead living in an unthinkably distant future still cared about them.

-James LaFond, August 17th, 2010, Baltimore, Maryland

Chapter 2
The Naked Man

"...his body was exhausted, his life-force spent,
...he knew that his mind had somehow grown larger,
he knew things now that an animal can't know."

-Gilgamesh

His claws are brittle. His stubby fangs do not protrude from his delicate jaw.

He grows no hooves, horns or antlers. But he stands tall and has hands to fashion and wield weapons against an enemy; to aide a loved-one, or to wrestle a rival. When he finds himself threatened and unarmed he instinctively clenches his hands around the tool that is not there and discovers a weapon—the fist.

Despite the multitude of ingenious weapons he has devised, the fist has fascinated and obsessed his kind since they first began to record their deeds. The raised fist is a universal sign of defiance. The clenched fist is a symbol of power and dominance used by leaders as diverse as the ancient God-King of Egypt, Amenhotep III, the medieval King Richard Coeur de Lion, American President Theodore

Roosevelt, and, the supreme tyrant of the industrial age, Adolph Hitler.

Even now, in the post-industrial nursery of 21st Century American Society, televised news programs treat us to boxing spectacles as varied as a Seattle police officer using boxing to defend himself against teenage girls, and a retired leader of the Vice Lords gang in Chicago using boxing instruction as a means to suppress street-fighting among young people.

Society is suspicious of the armed citizen, and largely indifferent to the unarmed fighter. Boxing has come to exist as a compromise between the combative individual jealous of his autonomy, and the mothering society, jealous of her authority. The fist that helped an ape rise from all fours, emerged as a symbol of power among the earliest conquerors, lingered as an instrument of honor through ages of armed terror, and might even, in some weaponless future, remain as a reminder to man of what he once was.

Here we sit wondering about ages-dead fighting men, in a world beyond what the first boxers would have conceived of as the-end-of-time, and ritual fist-fighting [boxing and MMA] remain a vibrant aspect of the human condition.

Chapter 3
The Cunning Hand: Adapting the Naked Hand to Ritual Combat

"...for the swift play of cunning hands."
—Quintus Smyrnaeus, *The Fall of Troy*

To undertake any technical study of boxing methods one must be able to identify and understand the various hand positions and configurations [henceforth "hand orientations"] utilized by boxers and fencers [fencing being a parent art to boxing]. Below is a study of the hand orientations and related ancient anatomical concepts discussed throughout this book, with notations on their origins and applications.

Caution: If the reader is a boxer he must understand that the use of the ungloved fist in a prize-fight is often different than with the use of a glove. If the reader is a practitioner of an Asian-based self-defense art he must keep in mind the fact that various uses of the empty hand that are effective for striking untrained aggressors and other self-defense practitioners are too hazardous to be employed regularly by a bare-knuckle prize –

fighter against incredibly tough and highly conditioned opponents who were often skilled at breaking hands.

Bare-knuckle fighters of the 18th and 19th centuries were often genetic freaks, sometimes selected by promoters because of such dubious feats as surviving a horrendous work-place accident. In such a climate, without gear or weight classes, normal athletes who relied on skill to survive in the prize ring, cultivated conservative techniques that maximized bone stabilization. Such popular modern self-defense strikes as the back-fist, ridge-hand, and vertical fist to the body are far too risky to be employed in the pit of horror that was The London Prize Ring, where bouts often lasted for hours.

Ancient boxing bouts were either conducted with little or no protective hand gear or with actual weaponry affixed to the hand. What is now the sport of modern boxing, was, in the ancient world and in the age of the London Prize Ring, simply a form of training and recreation.

The biomechanical discussions that address the illustrations below are wide-ranging and reference various arts; including possible weapon arts that might have encouraged these hand uses; modern arts, and the Greek arts that are the subject of the next volume.

Illustration A
The Cubit

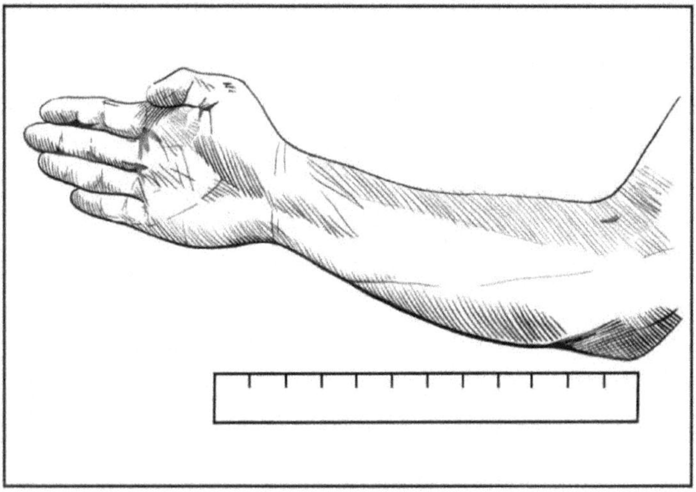

The ancients reckoned the hand from the elbow. A cubit, or hand-length, was the distance from a man's elbow to the tip of his fingers. [One supposes that ancient construction workers dreaded architects of unusual stature.] A criminal would be nailed to the Roman crucifix through the wrist, which was conceived of as a portion of the hand-length. Lygdamis of Syracuse, the first man to win the pankration [all-power-thing] at the 33rd Olympiad [648 B.C.], was said to have had feet a cubit long; that is the measure of a normal man's hand-length.

Illustration B
The Pugdon

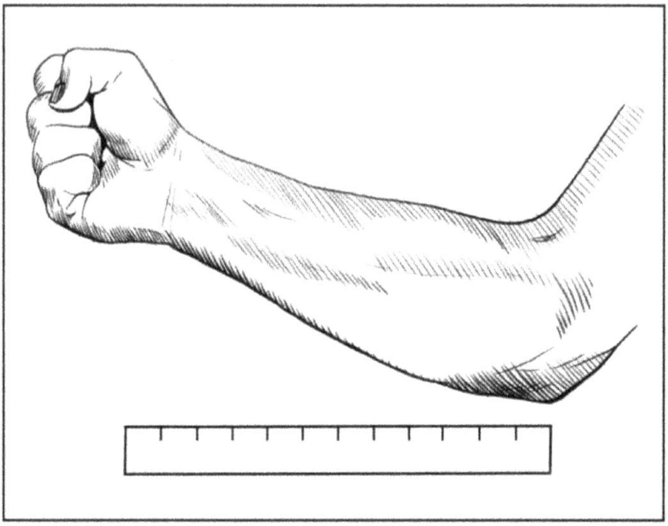

Knowing the hand to be useless without the nerves, muscles and ligaments of the forearm, ancient boxers protected the wrist with leather-straps and by other means, from an earlier date, and to a greater extent, than they did the actual business end of the fist. The pugdon or "fist-length" was the measure of a Greco-Roman boxer's arm from elbow to knuckle. It would be regarded with interest by ancient coaches and spectators in the same way that their modern counterparts now look at a fighter's reach [measured from fingertip to fingertip] and fist diameter, as a measure of punching potential.

Illustration C
The Vertical Fist

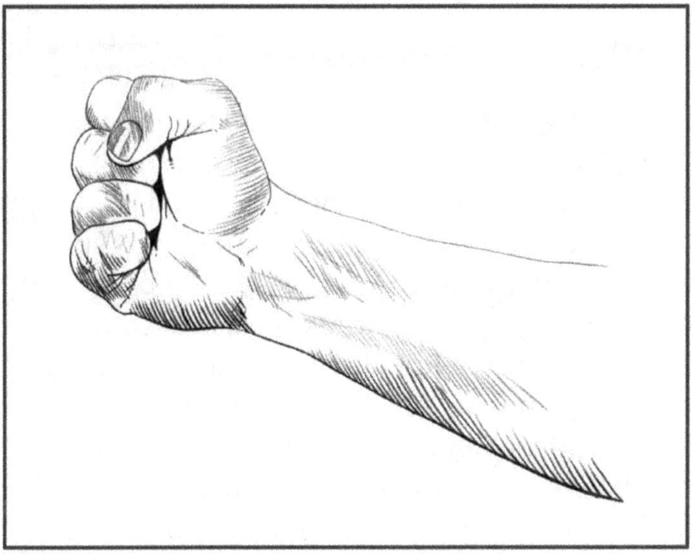

The thumb-up fist is based on gripping hafted [stick-mounted] weapons such as the spear and axe, as well as hand-held shields. This represents the first known fist presentation by a boxer, and persisted as the dominant hand orientation in western boxing through the 1890s. The primary advantage to punching with the fist in this position is thumb protection –no small concern for bare-knuckle and hand-strap boxers—when targeting the face. However, when applied to the body, as in modern Wing Chun gung fu, it puts the thumb and wrist at extreme risk of fracture, as these two light bones will eventually collide with the elbows of any decent boxer. For this reason vertical fist punches were used almost exclusively to access the face until the advent of the modern boxing glove.

A curious side-note on the dominance of the vertical fist and the absence of heavy punching bags prior to the gloved era may shed some light on the glacial pace of pre-modern boxing evolution. A heavy punching bag was never accepted by boxers until the gloved era because of damage to the thumb-side of the wrist caused by the downward force of a buckling bag. Greek boxers used light bags, London Prize Ring boxers used no striking equipment, and late19th Century American bare-knuckle and small-glove boxers used an adapted rugby ball called a "flying-bag" which developed into the speed bag and double-ended bag by the 20th Century.* The dreaded heavy bag that nobody liked to work on because it jammed the wrist, only weighed 10 pounds and was soft, being filled with horse hair, which was the same material used to stuff boxing gloves until the 1970s.

In an experiment conducted with Coach Dan Funk, during which the author punched mitts without wraps or other wrist support, the author was unable to tolerate throwing vertical punches with the two large knuckles when Coach Funk met the blow with a downward beat, as is common with many mitt drills to save the mitt-holder's elbows and shoulders. Wing Chun style three-knuckle punches [which were used effectively by big-handed genetic freak Jack Dempsey c.1920] did not impart this stress to the wrist joint. However, there is little evidence of the use of the three-knuckle punch in ancient and London Prize Ring boxing, and, even among gloved boxers competing with tapped hands, most modern hand breaks consist of a "boxer's fracture", which is the breaking of the two unanchored hand bones terminating in the two small knuckles.

A secondary use of the vertical fist was the delivery of a "Joe Frazier" or "Philadelphia-style" hook to the head. Vertical-fist hooks to the body would be very rare without thumb protection. In a bare-knuckle or small glove context the power-punch indicated by a vertical fist alignment is most likely the hammer-fist.

*Edwards, William. *Art of Boxing*, Brohan, 1888, pages 41-3
Donovan, Mike. *The Science of Boxing*, Fitzgerald, NY, 1893, pages 67-9
Fitzsimmons, Robert. *Physical Culture and Self-Defense*, Drexel Biddle, London, 1901, page 77-83

Illustration D

The Open Hand [cupped for protection of the digits]

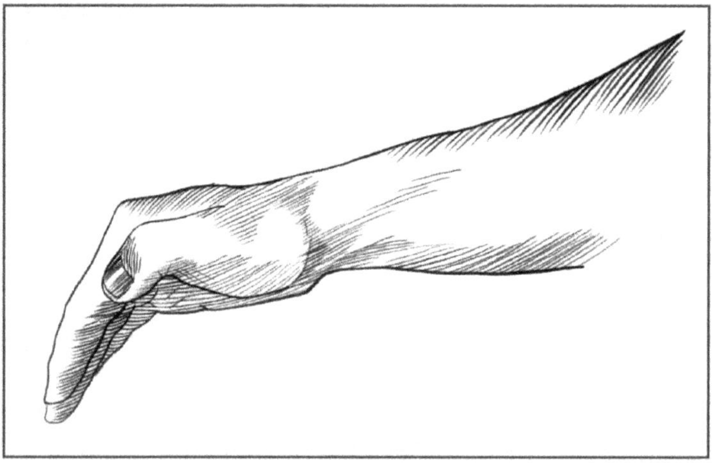

The open hand figures prominently in many forms of boxing [primarily Chinese boxing and kenpo] and certain types of fencing [most notably Filipino weapon arts], and in upright wrestling [such as sumo and Greco-Roman]. The *effective* use of open hand techniques by a boxer or fencer during the course of a prize-fight or duel generally denotes a level of skill equal to or greater than one's opponent.* Although boxers and weapon-fighters are usually taught numerous open-hand parries and more exotic counter-measures as novices, these are rarely employed effectively in actual combat. In fact, it is a rare thing to see a boxing match wherein a less-skilled fighter successfully parries, catches, measures, etc.; though the more skilled fighter will often take these liberties.

This disparity between training doctrine and actual practice is even more glaring in the contact weapon arts. Typically only one-in-ten stick fights will see an actual empty hand strike or disarming grab, even though practitioners of the Filipino weapons arts [who are the most avid members of the full-contact weapon-set] constantly indoctrinate themselves into believing that the "live" hand is just as important as the stick hand. Virtually all successful empty or "live" hand techniques are used against an overmatched fighter. In fighting with blunt steel machetes of knife and sword size the touted "live" hand has only made its presence felt in 3 out of 218 bouts.

These differences in training doctrine and actual combat application must be accounted for when considering the combat arts we will be examining as part of our exploration into the world of the ancient prize-fighter.

*This may simply be an indication of less-skilled [and generally less-experienced] fighters suffering the effects of combat stress, which impairs one's use of open hand [fine-motor] skills, thus encouraging a dependence on closed-fist [gross-motor] skills.

Illustration E
The Supinated Fist

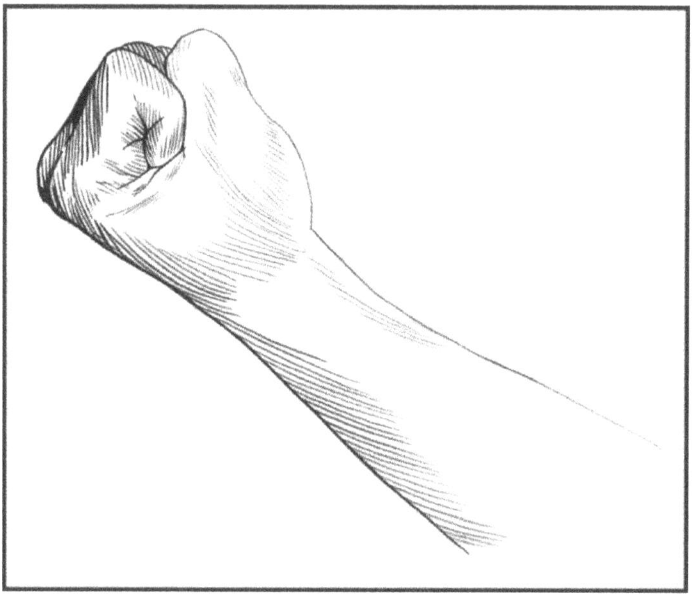

The palm-up fist is based on blade fighting, and its use is generally limited to specific targets [such as the eye-socket and groin]. Few boxers master even a single application of the supinated fist. This may come as a surprise to white-collar boxers and self-defense practitioners. After all, one reasons that since the uppercut is the 4th punch of the 4-punch arsenal of the modern boxer, it would be employed with regularity. Once again, doctrine and reality depart company.

The facts on the uppercut in modern boxing are as follows. It is the last of the four basic punches to be taught in the gym. It is often taught incorrectly. There is usually not a punching apparatus in the gym which a boxer may strike with an uppercut without injuring his wrist on the sensitive thumb-side. The standard uppercut bag is not too hard on the wrist, but is no good for other punches, and the uppercut is no good alone. It must be trained in combination with other blows, which is discouraged by the equipment generally available. Furthermore, most boxers are –thanks to the suction-like politics of amateur boxing—throne into the ring at local events before they have acquired the correct use of any of the angular blows [hooks, uppercuts and hybrid punches]. Less than one-in-ten competition-level boxers ever consistently employ the uppercut.

In ancient times and in the bare-knuckle era the uppercut was exclusively a head or groin punch. In the London Prize Ring it was only used by a fighter who had his man in a head-lock!

The uppercut however is a coveted punch, and it is not the only blow delivered with the supinated fist. The supinated jab, used rarely by modern boxers because of concerns with maintaining a high guard, was the most feared punch of the bareknuckle era. It was sometimes called "the special punch", and was utilized to drive the two large knuckles up into an opponent's eye-socket to strike the eye-ball directly and/or crack the orbit of the eye. Bare-knuckle fights often finished with one or both fighters having their eyes "hideously swollen out of their sockets". Despite its rare and uneven use throughout the history of ritual fist-fighting this fist orientation has been valued highly by gloved and bare-knuckle boxers alike.

One rare use of the supinated hand would be a hook thrown around behind the elbows into the ribs or armpit. Another rare blow would be a lateral hammer-fist to the head or a diagonal hammer-blow turned in on impact to damage the kidney.

Illustration F
The Pronated Fist

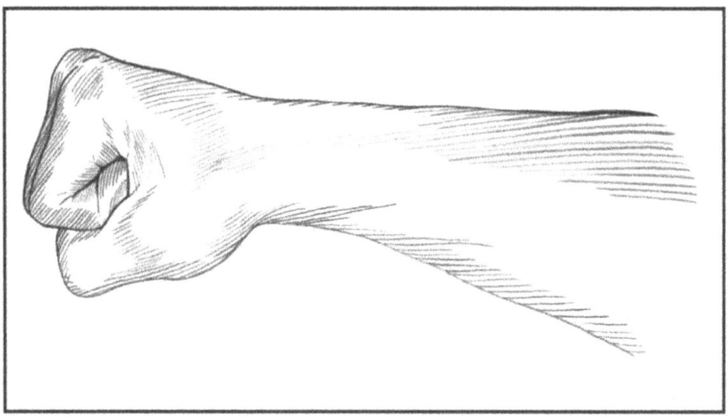

The use of the palm-down fist in ancient and modern boxing has been based on any of five types of weapon usage, enumerated below in order of their probable influence on punching development:

1. Punching with gloves and gauntlets
2. Punching with an arm-mounted [strapped] shield
3. Punching with a hand-held buckler [small punch-shield]
4. Thrusting from the outside with a blade
5. Hurling missiles [such as the dart or javelin]

The primary benefit to punching with the pronated fist is reach and power derived from rotating the shoulder into the blow. The primary deficit is risk of injury to the thumb, wrist and fingers when punching through or over an opponent's guard. Hence this has become the primary method of punching with modern boxing gloves. Above all pronated punching encourages strikes to the head. Bare-knuckle fighters generally confined the use of pronated punches to the body. This permitted the thumb to hide safely under the hand unexposed to elbow catches. It also covered the tucked chin with the rotated shoulder on one side. Exposing the skull in a bare-knuckle bout was not a big risk as no one wanted to crush their hand on it. Pronated punches to the jaw were usually not leads, but rear-hand finishing shots to the jaw set up by a vertical-fist jab. It should be noted that pronated punches thrown above the level of the puncher's own shoulder will force the wrist to bend and achieve poor energy transfer, unless the target [such as the jaw] has empty space below it for the clenched fingers to hang as the knuckles strike.

Curiously the only pronated jabs demonstrated in ancient Greek art are depicted as being thrown primarily by gods and mythic Lapiths, only once by an ordinary fighter. One additional and rare use of the pronated fist would be the hook to the back or kidney.

In rare instances a pronated fist may indicate the terminus of a hammer-fist strike thrown as a back-hand after missing a straight punch [a modern boxing foul], or after missing with a lead hook and then spinning backward to deliver a swinging blow with the rear hand [a foul blow –sometimes delivered with the elbow—of the 1880s and 1890s era of skin-tight gloves].

Illustration G
The Hyperpronated Fist

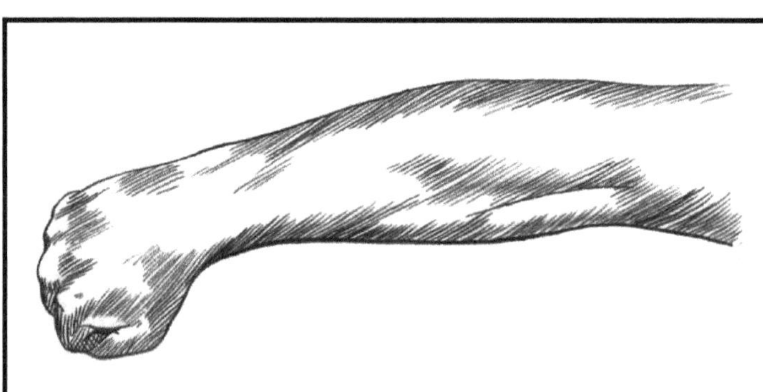

The use of the thumb-down fist [corkscrew punch] is known to be based on the use of the gloved pronated punch. It, may, however have been adopted by practitioners of now extinct forms of boxing based on the thrust of the sword or dagger. This fist orientation is only used to deliver a rare angular blow, and was a favorite among finesse-oriented knockout artists in the late 19th Century and early 20th Century. In modern times compact hard-hitting fighters sometimes [though rarely] use this fist orientation to apply extra force to taller fighters, via an overhand right, which is essentially a straight right delivered along a vertical arc. The primary exponent of the looping overhand right was heavyweight contender Ken Norton who campaigned in the 1970s, and used this punch to break the jaw of the great Muhammad Ali.

In the early 21st Century this fist orientation is used primarily by Hispanic fighters to throw a vicious cutting jab.

As with supinated punches, hyperpronated punches remain rare in competition because they cannot be practice extensively without injury to the punching limb –in this case the shoulder. People who have had torn rotator cuffs cannot even execute this blow in slow motion without pain.

Chapter 4
Dancing the Broken Dance: The Ten Basic Boxing Orientations or Guards

"At once each took his guard, and without fear
Held his hands high, dancing on tiptoe."
-Vergil, *The Aeneid*

Boxing is, quite literally, a broken dance. Each boxer enters the ring with the intention of setting the rhythm and pace of action –and ultimately breaking that rhythm in order to steal a beat from his opponent and gain total control. Through superior use of angles, rhythm, timing, and technique the boxer attempts to maintain a balanced position within striking distance of his opponent while at the same time denying the opponent an effective fighting position. The boxer who is capable of defeating more powerful fighters uses his art to maintain a superior combat orientation while dooming his opponent to fight from an inferior position.

The 10 orientations demonstrated below consist of 1 superior, 4 marginal, and 5 inferior orientations. The superior position is understood to be the central orientation flanked by 2 marginal positions to either side, 2 inferior positions to the left, and 3 inferior positions to the right. In many cases a fighter may have to shift to a marginal position to force or lure his opponent into an inferior one. The ten figures below should be read from the center out to either side. Leftward shifts in the boxer's guard close and ultimately limit his options. Rightward shifts open and ultimately expose his position. Very few fighters will operate across the entire spectrum, with most tending to drift back and forth across two or three guards.

This posture matrix was used by the author to evaluate the methods of ancient boxers preserved in—often rigid—art, such as carving, paintings and figurines. It is also useful in determining what types of martial activity, from weapon use to wrestling, may have influenced the preserved boxing methods. While the illustrated guide to boxing postures that follows is intended to provide a guide to analyzing a boxer on a biomechanical basis, it is also a tool for determining how his art may have evolved. The discussions of the postures below will therefore include comments on wrestling, kicking and weapon arts.

The Optimum Boxing Orientation

Illustration H: Superior, central

Balanced

As long as the boxer maintains this orientation toward his opponent he maintains leverage to throw all of his various punches with power while presenting a minimal target area.

Ideally he will put himself to [his] left of a squared opponent and fire power combinations to an exposed center as he moves safely off center away from the grapple, or he will drift right against the more linear opponent and put both of his hands to work against the other's lead hand.

Note: This is not the optimum "combat" orientation. Certain weapons—particularly dueling weapons—demand a narrower profile, and grappling generally demands a wider more lateral base. But remember, boxing is a compromise between dueling and wrestling.

Those weapon-fighters who favor this guard are aggressive single-stick fighters, stick and dagger fighters, and blade-fighters using a small punching shield in the rear hand. On the ancient battlefield such fighters constituted the light skirmishers or specialized flanking troops who tended to engage in a higher proportion of one-to-one duels than the heavy infantry of the line. In fact, the ownership of the region of the sacred precinct of Olympia in Greece was once decided by a duel between a slinger and an archer, who, it appears, fought it out by hand.

Leftward or Linear Orientations

A narrow linear profile is generally preferred by kick-boxers, defensive-minded single-stick fighters and duelists armed with a single blade. Weapon fighters who wield two identical weapons, such as double-stick or double-knife, tend to open up their guard.

Illustration I: Marginal, left

Narrow

While still presenting a minimal target area the fighter has pulled in his [right] rear foot and must now step out with that foot in order to strike effectively with the rear power hand to an opponent who has stepped slightly to the outside of his lead [left] hand. This is more effective as a mobile defensive orientation than as an offensive or static one.

Illustration J: Marginal, left

Linear [lined up]

When the boxer shifts his position so that his lead foot is directly in line with the opponent and his rear heal, he has lined up into a purely defensive orientation which does not permit effective use of the rear hand for offensive purposes without first shifting position. This position is favored by bare-knuckle fighters, defensive-minded kick-boxers, and fencers. This position does decrease the boxer's target area against linear attacks but leaves him open for hooking, sweeping, or slashing attacks that target his left.

The fact that a boxer or kick-boxer fighting from this orientation must open and close his stance to unleash his rear hand makes fighting from this position very demanding in terms of rhythm and timing.

Illustration K: Inferior, left

Crossed

A boxer in this position possesses no leverage for punching and his target area is increased to include portions of his back. A single misstep can bring a fighter dependent on a linear orientation into this trap.

Illustration L: Inferior, left

Turned [linear death]

Timid or clumsy fighters who get crossed tend to drift into this position when pressured. Tentative novice boxers in their first few sparring sessions tend to drift into the cowering position. This is often the final position of a linear-minded novice who has unsuccessfully engaged a laterally moving veteran.

Rightward or Lateral Orientations

The open guard was the standard heavy infantry posture in the ancient world, and those athletes with the most impressive battle records were wrestlers or pankratiasts [all-power-fighters] who served in the heavy infantry armed with a large shield.

Illustration M: Marginal, right
Open

This boxer is in position to throw power hooks with the rear hand but has opened up his target area. This is the kind of orientation favored by converted wrestlers and by heavy-boned brawlers who like to work on the inside. This man is typically easy to pick apart at long range and very dangerous to deal with at close range.

Illustration N: Marginal, right
Squared

This boxer has all targets open and only has leverage for hooking blows. The only points identifying him as a trained fighter are the crouch, the tucked chin, and the elbows held close to his ribs. From the boxer, to the kicker, fencer and wrestler, this is where everybody wants their man –ready to be taken down the middle. Being squared is how the offensive-minded fighter pushes his attack into a high-risk gamble, just as the defensive-minded fighter who lines up is playing his game to the brink.

Illustration O: Inferior, right

Sprawled [in the "peek-a-boo" guard]

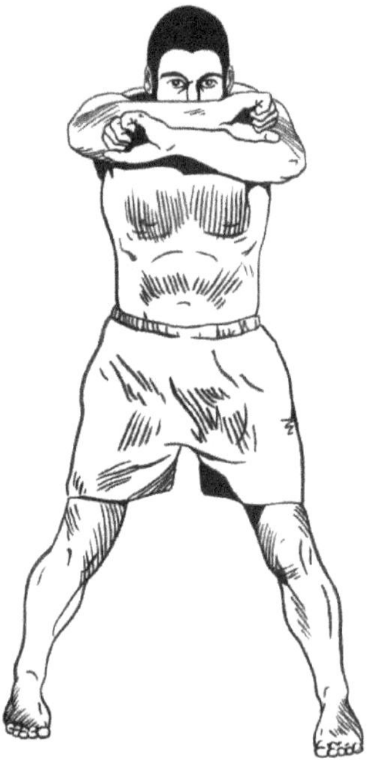

Short aggressive brawlers and older counter-punchers accustomed to fighting out of an open guard and protecting themselves with their elbows sometimes end up in this position when the action heats up against an active opponent. This guard was used by three notable late 20th Century boxers: Archie Moore, Ken Norton, and, during his come-back, George Foreman. This can be an effective counter-punching guard, and is best used to draw in "straight-up" linear boxers. This style tends to be disastrous against extremely strong fighters, and has fallen out of use in the 21st Century.

Illustration P: Inferior, right
Sprawled

A squared fighter who has gotten into serious trouble in the clinch will often extend the arms and pull back his feet. This denies all punching leverage but is actually better than being crossed. At least the fighter is in a better position to initiate a clinch with a boxer or avoid being taken down by a wrestler; and he is still facing his opponent. This is basically a counter-wrestling position. However, a taller boxer who becomes unbalanced by the body and chin attack of a shorter and/or more aggressive puncher will sometimes end up in this position as he attempts to right himself after bending too low from the waist while "weaving" between punches.

Illustration Q: Inferior, right

Standing still

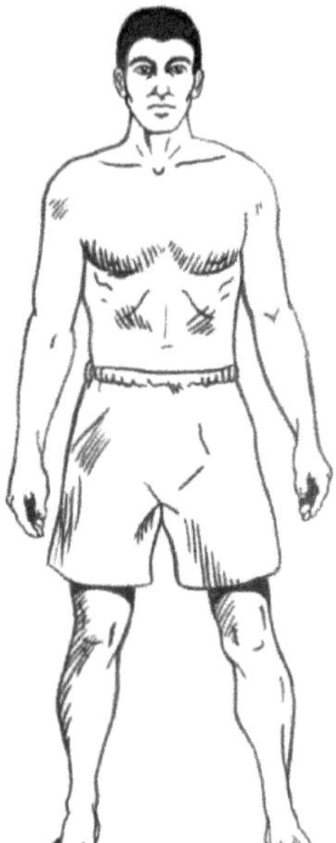

A squared or sprawled opponent who stands straight up is no longer in a fighting orientation. His targets are wide open and he has no immediate leverage for attack. However, unlike the turned fighter, he is at least facing his opponent and is therefore in position to adopt a fighting stance.

Conclusions

The stronger fighter obviously has the tendency to drift right where the immediate advantage to shifting his orientation are offensive in nature and the price for failure due to an extreme shift into an inferior position are not as severe as an extreme shift to the left. The weaker fighter is obviously compelled to play the leftward game which has a high defensive dividend but tends to put his whole tactical situation close to disaster as there are no benefits to crossing or turning. To play either the closed linear or open lateral orientation effectively the boxer must have excellent rhythm and timing. The boxer with the linear orientation must have superior lateral mobility, just as the boxer with the lateral orientation must possesses superior linear mobility. The key, quite obviously, is balance; and the best place to learn that is by fighting extensively from the balanced angled stance [Superior, central] at the centerpiece of this study.

Review of Leftward or Linear Boxing Postures

Superior

Oblique Narrow Linear

Inferior

Crossed Turned

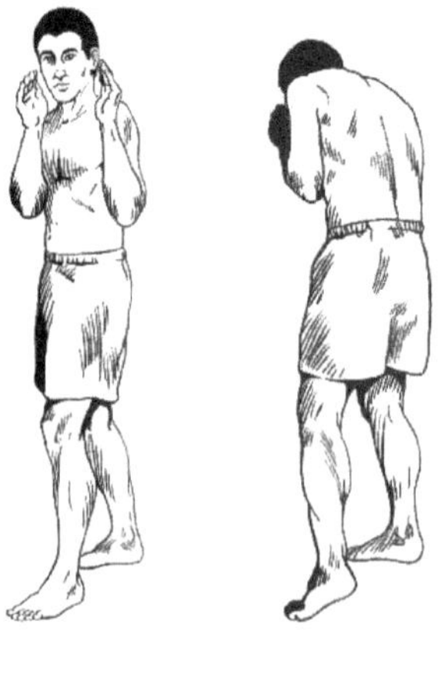

Review of Rightward or Lateral Boxing Postures

Superior

Open Squared Peek-a-Boo

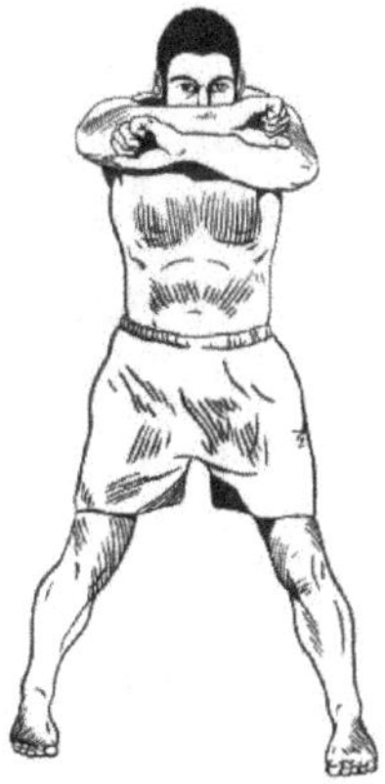

Inferior

Sprawled Standing

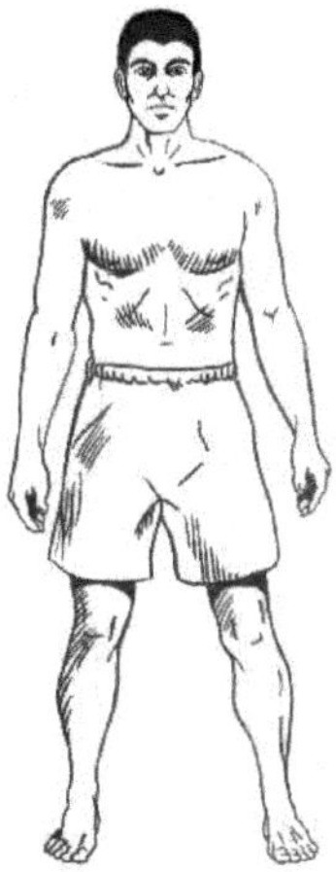

Chapter 5
Ghosts in Stone: Sacred Combat from *Gilgamesh* to *Goliath*, 2600 to 1000 B.C.

"Let us go, whore, take me to the holy sanctuary,
The abode of Anu and Ishtar,
Where Gilgamesh rules in perfect might and strength,
Where he controls people like a savage bull,
And I [Enkidu] shall challenge him and provoke him."

-*The Epic of Gilgamesh*

It is among the ruins of the long dead Near Eastern cultures of Mesopotamia, Crete and Egypt that one finds –carved into stone or ages-old baked clay—the first signs of boxing. We may never know for sure who the first boxers of antiquity were, or even where they fought. But we can form a fairly clear understanding of how and why these men boxed based on studies of later boxing traditions and of parallel cultural trends illuminated in the archaeological record.

The pursuit of ancient boxing knowledge leads the researcher into an odd dialogue with a few dozen nameless ghosts and a handful of forgotten gods. Despite the shadowy nature of our inquiry, and the very real possibility that nothing more than a faint echo might be drawn from such an effort, the surviving strands of this once rich tapestry of human action offer the patient researcher the promise of a true –if not total— understanding of the phenomena of ancient boxing and related forms of the prize-fighting arts.

Figure 1.
The Great Ziggurat
Babylon, Mesopotamia, c.560 B.C.

The first concrete [terracotta] evidence for ancient boxing was to be found amongst the remains of the ancient, and infamous, civilization of Babylon –apparently the first truly cosmopolitan city of the ancient world. Dated from the Old Babylonian period [c.2000 to 1595 B.C.] the find indicates that boxing was practiced as a sacred ritual by men of status. Such rites would have been conducted in the holy precincts of Babylon [or any Mesopotamian city] on, or in the shadow of, the city's central ziggurat [stepped pyramid], of which the great ziggurat of Babylon is the best known, being the inspiration for the biblical Tower of Babel.

This illustration is based on a reconstruction of the Great Ziggurat of Babylon commissioned by Nebuchadnezzar II [604 to 562 B.C.], which was itself a reconstruction of an earlier incomplete ziggurat. Towering hundreds of feet above the two-story sky-line of brick houses, a city's ziggurat pierced the sky like a sacred mountain, and would have dominated the visual field through every phase of a fighter's training; which would have been conducted in open courtyards, on flat roof-tops, and in the fields beyond the massive city walls.

Map 1. *The Rise of Boxing in the Ancient World*

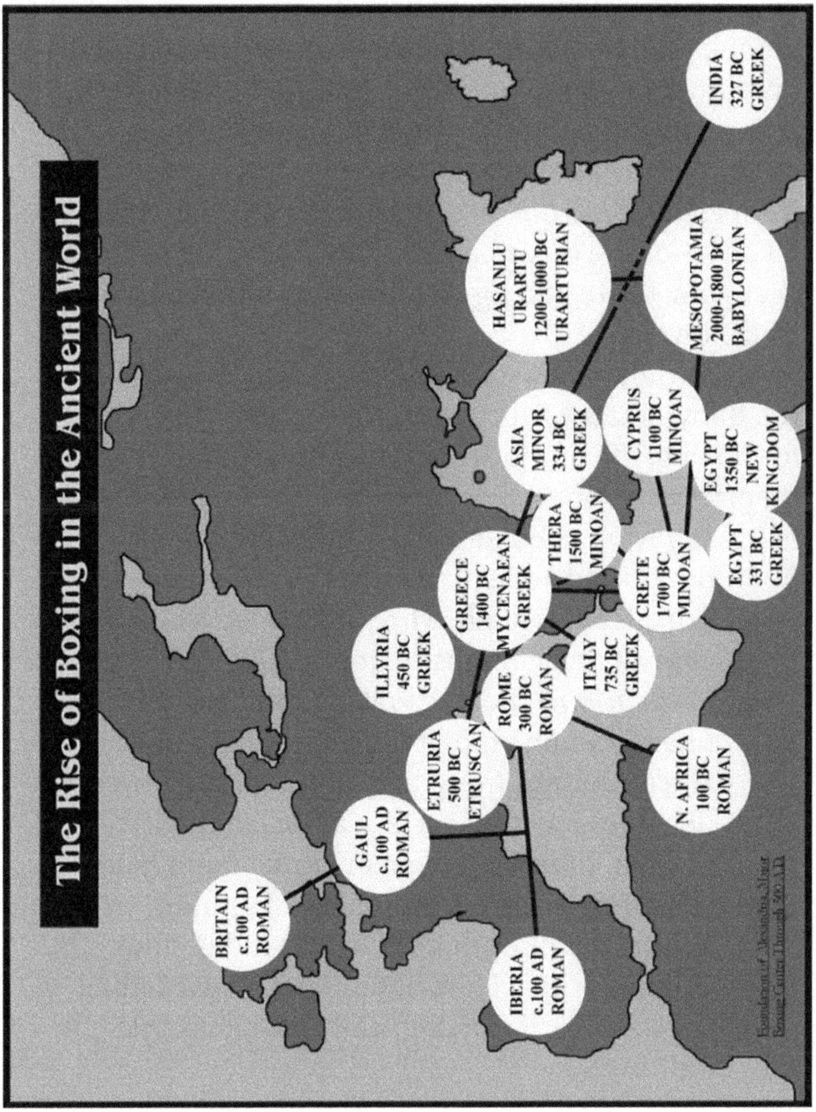

This map illustrates the spread of ancient boxing according to the theory of "diffusion", by which advances in human activity are thought to be unique and do not arise spontaneously among unrelated peoples, but must be spread through cross-cultural contact. Although ancient boxing certainly spread through cross-cultural contact from c.1350 B.C. onward, it remains unclear which –if any—of the three earliest known boxing centers [Babylon, Crete and Egypt] first developed a boxing tradition.

Although most boxing historians promote the Babylonian-Egyptian-Cretan-Greek progression for boxing, the author entertains two competing theories:

1. *Diffusion*.....Boxing was a martial ritual developed and spread by the same Indo-European nomads who introduced the war-chariot and composite bow c.2000 B.C.
2. *Cultivation*.....Boxing was a reoccurring phenomenon among the high civilizations of Mesopotamia, Crete and Egypt, influenced by developments in warfare associated with the gradual Indo-European encroachment, and resulting in the development of unique boxing traditions based on the indigenous combat arts of Mesopotamian belt-wrestling, Cretan sword-dueling, and Egyptian stick-fighting.

The author favors a combined theory. This is simply the supposition that the idea and practice of boxing was diffused along with the new technology brought into the world of the Middle Sea. But then, subject to local influences, the military elite, whether they be invaders, or those adopting the technology of the invaders for their own defense, cultivated their own unique boxing traditions.

A note on Indian boxing: although the Greeks did import their own arts into their Indian conquests, they found upon their arrival that Indian warriors were already involved in a boxing tradition, for which the prize was a wife. I was unable to uncover any additional information on the boxing-for-brides tradition. But it is noteworthy that this area of Northwestern India had been conquered by Indo-European tribes known as Aryans around the time that the areas under study in this book were adopting boxing traditions.

Note: Boxing seems to have spread from the area between the Caspian Sea and Black Sea, roughly the Iranian Plateau and the Caucasus Mountains, into the Middle East, and thence eastward to India and westward across the 'Middle Sea' and north into Europe, where it survived into modern times in Italy, Holland and the British Isles.

Chapter 6
Facing the Prime: The Origins of Boxing

"Warfare in the age of edged weapons required yet another vanished military quality...empathy with one's adversary...which would allow a man to look a stranger in the face and strike to fell him. Prizefighters, of course, possess this quality, whether learned or inherited and by reason of this fact alone have for the common man an intense, almost zoological fascination."

–John Keegan, *The Face of Battle*

Ironically enough, the history of ritual combat [encompassing martial arts and many ball sports] is very much the history of civilization. The very act of fighting an opponent according to set rules, as opposed to hunting him like an animal, is a "civilizing" attempt to limit violence. As we follow the story of boxing and related martial arts from the dawn of civilization into the modern age you will begin to appreciate boxing not as a "vestige of savagery" but as a powerful form of human expression that has ebbed and flowed with the fortunes of European culture and Western civilization.

Figure 2.
Origins & Evolution of Combat Sports

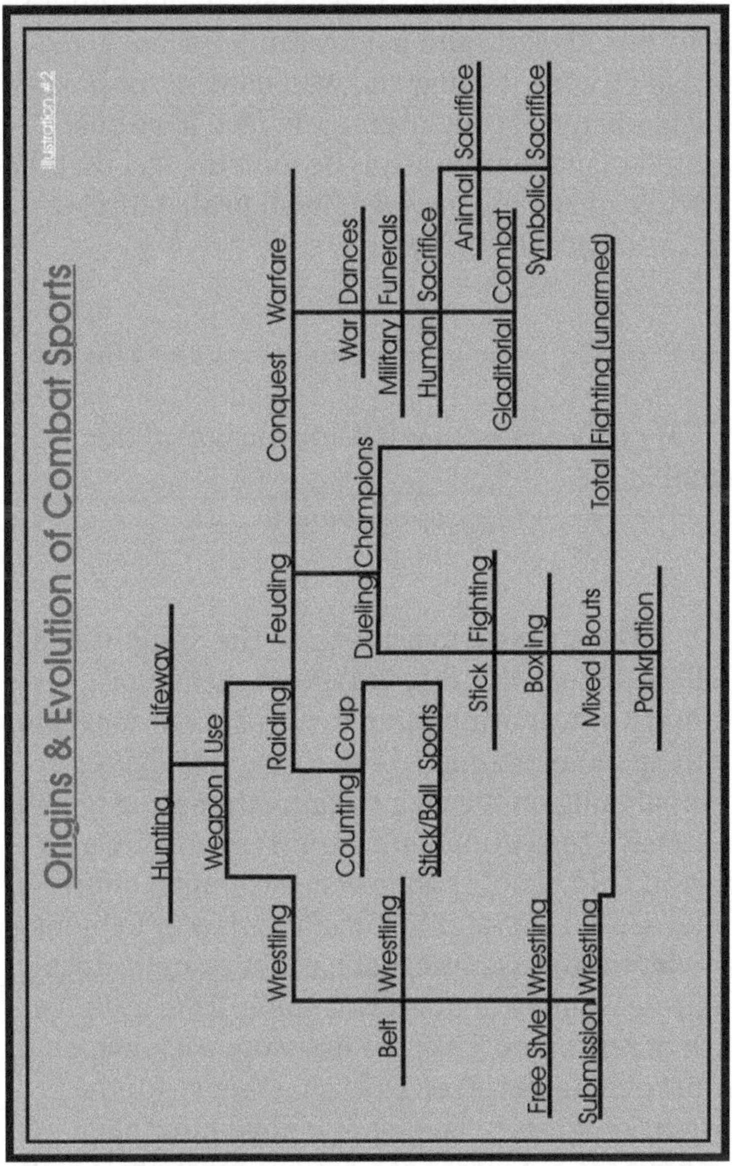

This table is a graphic representation of the author's theory on the evolution of ritual combat, specifically boxing [which includes, in the author's view, mixed bouts and pankration]. Unconnected parallel trends [boxing and war-dancing, or boxing and gladiatorial combat] may, in fact, have been related on numerous levels despite the fact that the practice of one did not lead [in all probability] to the practice of the other.

Rings of Dust: On Tracing the Origins of Boxing

"'My only achievement is for the lion of the sand!'"

—*The Epic of Gilgamesh*

The struggle to achieve on the margins of any field of endeavor is difficult. From the junior military officer attempting to pacify a border region with an under-strength unit, to a young fighter campaigning on the club circuit; attempting to force a decisive resolution with scant resources in a barren field of operations defies common effort. Likewise, an amateur historian's attempt to plumb the depths of a subject that has not been the focus of professional attention will suffer from a similar lack of resources. This, the first comprehensive effort ever undertaken to form a theory for the origins of Western boxing, is being undertaken without the resources of a major university, a staff of translators, or a team of grad students.

Therefore, if the aim of this author is to reconstruct a definitive account of the origins of Western boxing he is doomed to failure.

Instead, it is my stated aim to present and trace the various aspects of human action that may have resulted in the practice of boxing, as we know it, to emerge as a combat ritual important to ancient and modern Western societies alike. I have identified 18 specific threads that I regard as important to the emergence and perpetuation of boxing traditions. I will leave it to the reader to render a judgment as to the importance and relationship of these various threads. My advice on forming your own conclusion is this: imagine these threads forming a web without a center or a clearly defined perimeter.

The 18 aspects of human action related to the emergence of boxing traditions fall into three categories, and are outlined below in order of probable influence.

>Basic action patterns, upon which specific activities are dependent

>Specific activities, from which ritual fist-fighting would logically emerge

>Supportive activities, which *have* perpetuated boxing and *may have* formed a cause

	Basic	Specific	Supportive
1	Hunter	Wrestler	Soldier
2	Hero	Shield-bearer	Slave
3	Companion	Fencer	Priest
4	Shaman	Cowpuncher	Beer-drinker
5	The Prime	Citizen	Sailor
6	God-King	Dancer	Merchant

A Boxing Homeland?

Authors of modern or general boxing histories side with Mesopotamia or Egypt as the fount of all boxing, and then credit the Greeks with developing it and the Romans with eventually debasing it. Mesopotamia simply possesses the first concrete [terracotta] evidence. However, since the Mesopotamians were in contact with the Egyptians, Minoans, Hittites, Mykenaeans [proto-Greeks] and Urarturians, it is possible that they may have adopted or transmitted the practice of boxing *from or to* any or all of these cultures. There may even be an unknown common homeland of boxing. We simply do not know.

Hunter

"...Gilgamesh, with the deftness of a butcher,
Dealt the Bull of Heaven a deadly thrust
And plunged the sword between the nape and the horns."

–*The Epic of Gilgamesh*

The First Boxers

The hunt may be the fount of all things that modern man defines as human. This assertion is, of course, wide open for debate. However, hunting is the root of all martial activities from war to sport. Although examples of symmetrical warfare –such as the ritual engagements of the Aztecs and their rivals in pre-colonial Mexico in which captives for sacrifice were sought; and the gory slaughters of gorgeously costumed 18th century European "toy" soldiers in which kings literally played chess with human pawns –do dot the historic record, the vast majority of warlike acts are asymmetrical.

Symmetrical warfare may be described as "limited" or "ritual" in nature, while asymmetrical warfare is often described as "total" or "predatory". Hence mans' preferred method of war-making is an act of predation –generally consisting of the hunting of our enemies. The recent wars by the United States against Islamic nations and insurgencies are perfect examples of asymmetrical warfare.

When considering the origin of martial rituals one must understand that these rituals were developed by hunting societies as a method of expressing a rivalry short of committing genocide. Armed with spears and other hand weapons designed for dispatching large animals, hunting societies were compelled to develop a non-lethal means of determining dominance. A group dependent upon five able-bodied males to provide meat for the winter could scarcely afford to permit the two best spearmen to fight all-out over feeding or mating rights. Such a duel [probably resulting in the death of #2 hunter and the wounding of #1] could potentially result in an economic loss of 20 to 50%. For an isolated subsistence-level economy permitting such a duel would be group suicide.

Alternative methods for resolving such disputes had to be developed. Additionally these methods must reflect the recognized lethal capacity of the contestants. A mere game of chance which made no allowance for prowess would quickly be rejected. The victor, loser and witnesses of any such contest for primacy must be satisfied that the outcome of the contest would largely reflect the probable outcome of a no-holds-barred spear duel, or at least reward the better hunter. It seems that virtually all human societies settled on two methods of contest to determine primacy: wrestling and ball-play [originally skull-play].

Wrestling became the method for determining dominance within the immediate [local] group –the teen-age males of many American families still wrestle for dominance – while ball sports would determine dominance within the extended [related] group*. Of course "those other people", or "the non-people", or "the followers of the wrong god", would still be hunted like the animals they were perceived as being. However the dispute was resolved, hunting was the model and war the context. Think of, if you can, a sport that does not involve chasing or aiming –the key aspects of the hunt. Likewise, try to imagine a form of sport combat that does not require of its top practitioners both strength of body and keenness of mind–the key attributes required of the hunt-leader or war-chief. Of special interest is the *extreme lack of interest* in competitive ball-sports among the ancient Greeks who had a singularly fanatical devotion to ritual man-to-man combat, and a fatally fractious political life as an extended [related] group.

*My theory on ball-sports as martial arts must remain underdeveloped in this work. A few observations: Lacrosse and polo [originally played with a skull?] appear to be ball sports which were specifically adapted as training for war; the Duke of Wellington's famous saying about his troops' excellent performance at the battle of Waterloo being related to the ball-playing experience of their officers; and the obvious conquest metaphors in American football from armor to taking territory.

Hero

"So Gilgamesh said to Enkidu:
'The terrible Humbaba lives in the forest:
So let us kill him, you and I,
And remove evil from the face of the earth...'"
-*The Epic of Gilgamesh*

A hero or heroine is that person which represents the aspirations of a people in the undertaking of deeds which put them at great risk.

The Greek word hero is first used in literature to describe tribal strongmen and champions by Homer in his *Iliad*. Initially the hero would be the hunter who was willing and able to enter a darkened cave and eject some monstrous predator from its lair so his folk could have shelter. This figure would eventually become the duelist who represented his army between the battle-lines, the athlete who represented his people in sacred contests, and finally an intermediary between humanity and the gods once he had passed on. In retrospect heroes do not appear as altruists sacrificing for the common cause so much as supreme egotists attempting to achieve immortality–as many did.

In our own prosperous, largely risk-free age, the hero has become a source of entertainment. As an athlete, comic-book character, or motion-picture protagonist the hero is merely a vehicle for the vicarious thrill-seeking of a couch-bound society; and as such he is richly rewarded, becoming far more wealthy than heads-of-state and corporate CEOs. In attempting to develop an appreciation for the ancient ideal of heroism the modern mind is caught between the image of ordinary people taking a once-in-a-life-time risk–such as rescuing a neighbor from a burning house—as reported on the nightly news, and the washed-out celebrity hero packaged on DVD. The relevance of the hero to early man lays somewhere between the ordinary and the ridiculous in modern terms.

Ancient literature consistently depicts the hero as a victim of tragedy, yet the most powerful men of the ancient world continually attempted to emulate the heroic deeds attributed to these mythic figures, knowing full-well that the consequences would tend toward the tragic. When we try to appreciate the motivation of ancient warriors and prize-fighters, don't think in terms of the boy next door attempting to emulate a sports, comic-book or movie hero as a blue-print for little-league success; but instead, of a missionary putting his or her life on the line in some hellish third-world ghetto. In other words, of someone taking an extreme risk for what they believe in.

Many will take issue with this contention that the ancient hero was a spiritual beacon akin to the crucified messiah of a world religion. The idea might be easier to swallow if we stop thinking like a member of a 250-million-person state, or a 1-billion-person faith; but rather as a member of a band of some 5 families who must trust to their men for protection—men who are emotionally dependent on a recognized leader; so recognized for his willingness and ability to routinely take extraordinary risks on their behalf.

The need for small warring societies to institutionalize a method for developing a cult of extreme risk-taking in order to insure that some men would always be emotionally capable of putting it *all* on the line, forms the root of the western martial tradition, encompassing contact ball-sports, dueling, war-fighting and unarmed prize-fighting.*

The term Olympian, now used to describe elite athletes, was once applied to gods alone.

*Leick, Gwendolyn. *The Babylonians: An Introduction*, Routledge, London, 2003, pages 25-30

Leick offers a succinct analysis of interstate brutality and civil control in old Sumer carried out by strongmen whose authority was based on "divine right". The scribes of these tyrants –to whom the historian is deeply indebted—were little more than propaganda ministers, extolling the power and virtue of their boss, who was typically depicted as dutifully fulfilling the will of the state god through conquest and administration

Companion

"'He passed away, and I wept for him day and night.
I mourned him for six days and seven nights,
Cherishing the hope that he would live again
Through the abundance of my tears and mourning,
And I refused to hand him over to the grave.'"
—*The Epic of Gilgamesh*

Perhaps the first and best reason for a primitive society to develop violent or bloody rituals is to appease or honor the spirit of a brother-in-arms. The type of bond formed between men who share the risks of the hunt and war is profound. Any such rite must involve bloodshed as early man recognized blood as the very stuff of life, often providing even more significance to its loss than would a modern medical practitioner*. Honoring one's dead companion with blood is probably an outgrowth of the practice of blood covenants; that is becoming blood brothers through consuming or mixing one-another's blood. From this practice of acknowledging the transfer of one's martial essence via the mixing or consumption of blood, funerary practices would have evolved along the following lines:

1. Sacrifice of a prey animal to appease the ghost of the hunter.
2. Consumption of the deceased [in part, at least] along with the sacrificed animal in order to keep his essence among the living.
3. The eating of an honored enemy's special part in order to capture his power.
4. The sacrifice of enemy captives [slaves] to satisfy the ghost's vengeance.
5. Sacrifice of captives by way of a combat to the death which spares half the slaves for future use while honoring the departed warrior's fighting spirit.
6. Sacrificial combat between two companions of the departed, with the victor retaining the possessions of the loser and the departed, thus keeping assets within the tribe which otherwise would have been buried with the dead man.

7. Sub-lethal, yet bloody, dueling [stick-, first-blood edged-, and fist-fighting] between companions, thus appeasing the ghost and sparing all sacrificial assets, that otherwise would have been lost to the grave, for use by the living.

The obvious trend here, as with most religious traditions, is the setting aside of an increasingly larger portion of the sacrificial stakes for the use of the living, with the devotions to the dead becoming ever more symbolic. In those periods of antiquity marked with known and significant occurrences of ritual combat [2600 B.C. – A.D. 551] only the spirits of the most powerful departed souls [heroes, gods, deified rulers] were honored with sacrifices of human blood –primarily through sacred athletic competition and gladiatorial combat.

Sacrifice via ritual combat would have had special appeal to the earliest warrior societies, since the sacrificial act itself would have actually consisted of a practice that had been regularly engaged in by the departed. One must not forget that our very first record of a boxing match recorded in literature is to be found in Homer's *Iliad*, at the funeral of Patroklus, held by his companion Achilles.

*Tannahill, Reay. *Flesh and Blood, A History of the Cannibal Complex*, Dorset, NY, 197

Figure 3.
A Bloody Wake
Illustration of Author's Theory on Boxing Origins, Gorgan Region, Iran, 2250 B.C.

Two comrades of a slain warrior of a semi-nomadic tribe honor his warrior-spirit: one by conquering his opponent in boxing and taking the departed man's place –and possessions—in life; the other by shedding his blood to appease the lingering ghost.

Shaman

"...Jacob was left alone, and a man wrestled with him there till daybreak. When the man saw that he could not get the better of Jacob, he struck him in the hollow of his thigh, so that Jacob's hip was dislocated as they wrestled. The man said, 'Let me go for day is breaking,' but Jacob replied, 'I will not let you go unless you bless me.' The man asked, 'What is your name?' 'Jacob,' he answered. The man said, 'Your name shall no longer be Jacob but Israel, because you have striven with God and mortals, and have prevailed.'"

—Genesis 32: 24-8

The shaman [spiritual medium] of a tribe is often an aged or otherwise odd personage, interceding on behalf of the hunters with the animal spirits. In many cultures his status as a medicine-man, witch-doctor or other brand of visionary is based on his warrior status, and he could be expected to possess special fighting methods, perhaps based on animal behavior, as he is a recognized intermediary between the tribe and the beasts.* The shaman might be involved with the ritual abduction of the newly adolescent boy from the quarters of the women and children; and also – as the keeper of arcane lore—be consulted as a wrestling coach by young bucks seeking to unseat the reigning wrestling champion. Finally, being a status member of the tribe with significant leisure-time on his hands, the spiritualist might be tempted to experiment with combat methods.

It is this author's opinion that wrestling as a spiritual meditation, along with the imitation of animal fighting methods, and the sacrificing of animals which would net much anatomical knowledge, makes the primitive spiritualist a fine candidate for first wrestling guru –and wrestling is most certainly the bedrock of ritual combat.

Of course, later involvement in martial sports by monks and priests is an obvious indication that their predecessors, the tribal shaman of prehistory, had some hand in the growth of ritual combat. Two further indications are the association of massage therapy with training for ritual combat among the Greeks, Romans and Chinese, and the amazing story of the Aleut pressure-point wrestlers as related by Richard Rudgley in his fascinating book *The Lost Civilizations of the Stone Age*:**

"...in the fighting techniques of the Aleuts...used both in the sport of wrestling and in actual combat...in part derived from their observations of fighting animals...it is plausible that the Aleuts and Alaskan Eskimo groups share a tradition with the Chinese that would have its routes in the prehistoric era...a prehistoric origin for the acupuncture/fighting technique complex seems to be lent support by the great popularity of wrestling among the Mongolians and the various peoples of north-eastern Siberia..."

When discussing the shaman we are also identifying the earliest medical practitioner—the healer. In the 20th Century boxing gym that was the trainer, more specifically the cut man, who was often just as good at tending to a battered face as any licensed doctor. Also, we must not shy away from using Asian martial arts as a model for our inquiry. Asian boxing arts demonstrate some technical and cultural similarities to Western arts, making them legitimate study models. Among traditional Chinese boxing practitioners the sifu [father-teacher] also doubles as a healer, formulating his own ointments and prescribing and applying various treatments for his student's injuries.

*Utley, Robert M. *The Lance and the Shield: The Life and Times of Sitting Bull*, Holt, NY, 1993, pages 10-37
Utley does a superb job of detailing the cardinal virtues of the Lakota warrior.

**Rudgley's assertions in this area are based on the work of Anthropologist William Laughlin, a specialist in Aleut studies. Although Laughlin is quoted extensively, no work of his is listed in the bibliography, so I must assume an interview or private correspondence is the source.

The Prime

"The young men of Uruk, angry and beaten, stayed in their lodgings...
'His lust has not left a virgin to her mother
Nor a warrior's daughter nor a hero's betrothed.'"
—*The Epic of Gilgamesh*

The prime male, the alpha, boss, jefe, honcho, etc. is the focus of prize-fighting psychology. To this day the single most feared, desired, hated, envied and misunderstood sports figure is the world heavy-weight boxing champion. [This distinction is now shared in the 21st Century with his MMA counterpart.] Although he has come to prominence as a member of the most underpaid sport, he, himself earns more per contest than the most exalted stars of the highest paying ball sports on earth. He is the ultimate man or boogieman depending on your point-of-view. He, however, cannot be ignored. Even when he is an obscure character for reasons of personality [Larry Holmes] or the most outrageous character for reasons of behavior [Mike Tyson] he receives more independent attention from the common man's modern prophet [the sports reporter] than any more well-known or more accomplished ball-player in existence.

All dominant American heavyweight champions have been *extreme* womanizers; with young women literally lined up at hotel-room doors seeking an audience of the most intimate kind with the king of the most brutal sport still practiced by man. The more feared by powerful mainstream male society [Jack Johnson, Sonny Liston, Muhammad Ali, Mike Tyson], or the more respected for their shear toughness and masculinity [Rocky Marciano, Evander Holyfield] the more these men have been sought after by women. Women have often been their downfall with Johnson and Tyson both being imprisoned for what they took as ordinary relations with women. Even contenders are engulfed with female desire. When young Tommy Morison announced that he had tested positive for HIV a hotline set up in his hometown for women who had been intimate with him received over 2000 responses!

In fact, any fighter worth the label has experienced the seduction attempts of female gym-goers, the mothers of young boxers, and even women who have never seen a bout but who are attracted by the mystique of a man who trains for and engages in combat.

Any reading of romance novels, marketed for perfectly normal modern women, betray the female fascination for men willing to fight.* A modern male escort enjoys increased appeal when prospective clients are told he is a former boxer, just as Roman gladiators and trainers were eagerly sought after as companions by the richest women in Rome.

And, to take that final leap into the distant past to see strongmen as the objects of feminine seduction we need only look at the four greatest literary works of antiquity:

The Epic of Gilgamesh in which Enkidu is seduced by the prostitute and Gilgamesh pays dearly for resisting the charms of a goddess;

The Old Testament, in which Samson is seduced by Delilah;

The Iliad, in which a years-long war is fought for the possession of the beautiful Helen, and the war is nearly lost when Agamemnon and Achilles feud over the possession of a slave girl [There were a lot of slave girls. This chick must have been something!];

The Odyssey, in which Odysseus is seduced by the goddess Circe...

Yes indeed, to the cynical observer prize-fighting really does seem to be about one thing and one thing only: establishing mating rights and attracting a harem much like the chest-thumping and bull-rushing of the African gorilla.

*Anderson, Catherine. *Sweet Nothings*, Onyx, NY, 2002, pages 429-34

God-King

"...it used to be the regular custom with the Shilluk to put the king to death whenever he showed signs of ill-health or failing strength. One of the fatal symptoms of decay was taken to be an incapacity to satisfy the sexual passions of his wives, of whom he has very many...but even while he was yet in the prime of health and strength he might be attacked at any time by a rival and have to defend his crown in a combat to the death."

—Sir James George Frazer, *The Golden Bough*

Kingship of a tribal society sounds a lot like the life of a modern American heavyweight boxing champion. Jack Johnson, Rocky Marciano, Muhammad Ali, Mike Tyson and Evander Holyfield where among the most socially dominant boxers of the 20th century, were all notorious womanizers, and fought eagerly anticipated championship battles in which their opponents almost always sought a knockout victory. Not only is the KO in boxing the perfect ritual metaphor for death-in-combat, but a KO visited upon the reigning heavyweight champion [king-of-boxing] has almost always resulted in the "death" of that fighter's boxing career. And, not coincidentally, when fighters such as Tyson and Holyfield stage a comeback they are cast by the media [our modern pop-culture witch-doctors] as either a ghost or shade of his former self [Tyson], or as a heroic miracle-man like Holyfield, who has actually been described by commentators as having "resurrected himself".

Although the institution of kingship in the ancient near east was most certainly based on warfare, there were quite possibly exceptions; such as the shadowy kings of Crete who may have been dominated by the priestesses of the great temples. Such a situation would entail a limited term of kingship, at the end of which the king would be required to play the ascending hero as he was sacrificed [ostensibly on behalf of the people, but more likely to insure the power of the priesthood]*.

However, at some point in history, it was inevitable that a doomed puppet king would take measures to insure his survival. This could take the form of substituting himself with a temporary king [king-for-a-week, with all the perks of office, including that last-minute promotion to companion of the undying goddess!] in the days leading up to the sacrifice, or taking a more direct role as a wrestler, boxer, or duelist who would fight a ritual combat against a temporary co-king; which would net the gods their royal sacrifice through, choke, knockout, or kill-stroke.

In considering the sacrifice of a temporary king as a possible origin of ritual fist-fighting we must abandon thoughts of such an origin in patriarchal Mesopotamia. If the [symbolic or mortal] passing of a temporary king was indeed an important current in the rise of boxing than the island of Crete, dominated by the goddess, is where one must look for further clues. [see Chapter 9].

In his doomed role the king would be acting as the most advanced of the seven forms of hero: The Ascender**. If not, then boxing is simply imitating life, and providing a brutal metaphoric link with the past. Never forget that the kings of boxing are not permitted to reign into their old age, symbols as they are of the vitality of their art. Furthermore, these kings virtually never permit themselves the luxury of retirement, choosing defeat [athletic death] instead.

*Campbell, Joseph. *Historical Atlas of World Mythology,Volume II: The Way of the Seeded Earth, Part 1: The Sacrifice*, Harper & Row, NY, 1988, pages 36-9

Of particular interest is the raised hand of the sacrificial victim similar to the sign given by defeated Greek athletes and Roman gladiators, the Mayan ball game after which the losing team leader is beheaded, and the spiritual significance of torture among North American tribes similar to the ancient Greek regard for agony.

**Campbell, Joseph. *The Hero with a Thousand Faces,* Princeton, Princeton New Jersey, 1972, pages 315-64

Wrestler

"The two grappled in combat,
And struggled and lowered and roared like two wild bulls;
They destroyed the pillar of the door and the wall trembled.
Gilgamesh and Enkidu wrestled like two wild bulls.
But when Gilgamesh, bracing his foot on the floor,
Bent over and threw Enkidu,
The heat of his fury cooled and he turned away to leave."

—*The Epic of Gilgamesh*

Wrestling is the oldest martial art. 20,000 year-old wall paintings of men in recognizable wrestling postures decorate a cave in the south of France. Wrestling is certainly a dominance/virility ritual that probably began as a way of settling mating disputes. The bull -idealized as a symbol of virility throughout the ancient near east—figures prominently in the mythology of wrestling champions: Gilgamesh and Enkidu wrestling the Bull of Heaven; Herakles subduing the mad bull of Poseidon in his seventh labor; Theseus and the Minotaur; the tale of Milo lifting the calf as a daily strength exercise as it grew into a bull; of Milo and a rival strongman devouring an entire bull...

The link with the bull and wrestling is obvious and deep. Furthermore, the fictional boxing champions of antiquity typically fought for a prize bull; a warrior's shield was traditionally crafted of seven layers of bull's hide; and a boxer's gauntlet in the Hellenistic and Roman period consisted of seven layers of bull's hide. The bull was a sacred beast, seven a sacred number, and the practices of wrestling and boxing sacred rituals.

On a more primeval level wrestling is laden with symbolism: the clinch symbolic of battle; the throw symbolizing conquest; the pin positioning the victor for rape; and the choke-out clearly mimicking death.

Beyond the obvious symbolic link with boxing, wrestling is a logical precursor to ritual fist-fighting for various reasons:

1. Being the first unarmed fighting method, succeeding empty hand arts would have been influenced –at least in their formative stage—by its conventions, such as facing off, fighting on a specially prepared surface, and wearing clinching belts such as the boxers in the *Iliad*.

2. Upright Greco-Roman style wrestling discourages ground-fighting but encourages slapping and butting tactics, and hence set the stage for boxing in Babylonia, ancient Greece, and 17th century England.

3. Wrestling inculcated the idea that man should settle disputes and determine dominance within their peer group without recourse to weapons.
4. Wrestling tends to disappoint man's thirst for blood-sports, making boxing the logical next step in the sanguine balancing act that is ritual combat.

Shield-Bearer: Shield Use and Punching Origins

"...after having stopped the Blow with his left Arm, which is a kind of Buckler [small punching shield] to him, he may have the more Readiness and greater Power of stepping in with his right Hand's returning Blow."

—Captain John Godfrey, on boxing, from *A Treatise Upon the Useful Science of Defence*

Just as the lethality of the hunter's spear certainly suggested ritualistic adaptation of the human child's natural impulse to grapple as a sub-lethal alternative to spear-dueling, the shield very likely suggested fist-fighting to the shield-bearing spearmen of early antiquity. The author's contention in this area is based firstly on the fist/shield comparisons often made by fencing masters, and secondly on experimentation.

In 2002, after a few years of heavy fencing practice with blunt knives, bamboo swords, and rattan sticks, the members of ***Modern Agonistics*** [of which the author is the cofounder and coordinator] began to experiment with various types of shields. The premise behind the entire program was that it would be quicker to arrive at ancient weapon fighting technique through blind experimentation than through painstaking deconstruction of surviving modern fencing forms. All of the experimentation was full-contact, with minimal gear, and was competitive, often fought for the fencers' beer money! There was no choreography.

The shield-fighting experiments yielded 3 significant results:

1. Short oaken cut-and-thrust swords of the ancient type were found to be heavily dependent on the shield. In fact, in more than half of the bouts the use of the shield was judged by the fighters to have had more influence on the outcome of the combat than that of the sword.
2. The various shield designs demanded more specialized techniques than that of the sword. For instance, a fighter who was good with a short sword usually did reasonably well with a long sword or a knife. But that same fighter would face serious hurdles adapting to the use of a new type of shield. As shield structure is so specialized that specialization of use becomes a prerequisite for success, fighters soon began to "push the envelope" to get the most out of their shield,

which resulted in a wide variety of offensive uses –mostly punching.

3. Fighters who had trained or competed as boxers always demonstrated shield superiority in small-shield [buckler] and sword contests, even when these same fighters were found wanting in sword use.

The practitioners in these contact experiments were all surprised and impressed by the utility of various shields, especially the small shields. In July of 2003, when ***Modern Agonistics*** fighters began dueling with dull machetes –similar in size and quality to ancient small swords—punching with the shield became even more decisive; leading the author to believe that ancient fighting men valued the punch *before* and *beyond* boxing.

Fencer: Stick-fighting, Swordsmanship and the Sweet Science

"Fig was the Atlas of the Sword, and may he remain the gladiating Statue!"

—Captain John Godfrey, on the first modern boxing champion, from *A Treatise Upon the Useful Science of Defence*

Those many and varied methods of fencing practiced by man the world over have, on some few occasions, resulted in the development and practice of fist-fighting traditions. Despite the fact that every culture has had a wrestling tradition and the vast majority have developed fencing traditions [and generally abandoned these with the advent of firearms technology], only a very few cultures have independently developed a boxing tradition. Below, listed in chronological order, are those early boxing traditions which this author believes to have been indigenous; that is arising independently without certain knowledge by the originators of an earlier similar tradition among ancestors or neighbors.

Known Indigenous Boxing Traditions

1800 B.C. Babylonian
1700 B.C. Cretan
1350 B.C. Egyptian
1200 B.C. Greek
1000 B.C. Urarturian [possibly under Babylonian influence]
500 B.C. Indian [possibly as ancient as proto-Greek boxing]
200 B.C. Chinese [horned-helmet wrestling, possible origin of Chinese boxing]
A.D. 700 Ireland [possibly under Romano-Breton influence
A.D. 1400 Okinawan [possibly under Chinese influence]
A.D. 1500 Thai [possibly under Chinese or Indian influence]
A.D. ? Oceanic [independent Pacific Islander traditions]

The search for a common thread linking cultures that develop boxing traditions nets two answers: recent conquest [Babylon, Egypt and Greece] and limited isolated territory [island living; Crete, Ireland, Oceana, Okinawa]. From this point in our inquiry it becomes necessary to leap forward to the rebirth of boxing in the west in search for parallels.

The islands of Ireland and Britain, the war-torn Netherlands, and feud-ridden Northern Italy all hosted the rebirth of boxing between 700 and 1600 A.D. In each case these fistic institutions were promoted by fencing masters or in opposition of fencing by community leaders as a sub-lethal alternative. Leaping back in history to 750 B.C., one finds in Homer's *Iliad*, at the funeral games of Patroklus, the putting down by Achilles of a possible duel between Little Ajax and Idomeneus over the conduct of the chariot race.

Further, when considering the fencing connection to boxing look to the exceedingly warlike tribes of Eastern North America who were renowned wrestlers and warriors with no fencing tradition to speak of, who [consequently?] failed to develop a boxing tradition*. Of course the type of fencing usually practiced by pre-modern people is simple stick-fighting–which just happened to be the rage in England and Northern Italy at the time when boxing emerged in those areas. For a final parallel the earliest boxing hand-gear [especially in Crete] is similar to common forms of fencing hand-gear.

Moreover, boxing shares more body-mechanics with fencing than with wrestling, and in its modern form is a direct descendent of fencing.

*Eckert, Allan W. *A Sorrow in Our Heart: The Life of Tecumseh*, Bantam, NY, 1992, pages 156-8, 372-3, 641,

Eckert describes Tecumseh behaving with predatory zeal when he dispatches a fellow warrior with his war club –there is no facing off, just quick death, even when it is a social dispute among members of an allied war-party. The running of the gauntlet by Simon Kenton and others also points to a purely predatory appreciation of weapons with one party being beaten by numerous armed parties. Also, the Amerindian practice of Lacrosse [Little Brother of War] and of counting coup, points to the appreciation of weapons as having to do exclusively with predatory group actions.

Cowpuncher: Cattle-Herding, Bull-Worship and Animal Abuse among Boxers

"The Bull of Heaven came down to earth
And began to spread terror and fear."
—*The Epic of Gilgamesh*

Boxing—coincidently or not—appears in ancient Mesopotamia, Crete and Egypt within 200 years of the appearance of chariot warfare. Indeed, the very first literary account of boxing in Homer's *Iliad* is obscured within the epic by the lavish attention paid to the chariot-handling exploits of heroes far more violent than those who contest for the prize bull in boxing. Perhaps it is simply the result of a generalized trend toward more extreme violence in the ancient world that wrestling was eclipsed by boxing at the same time that the hero on foot was superseded by the chariot-mounted bringer of death.

Snorting steeds raking the earth with their shod hooves enhance the menace of the warrior's image every bit as much as identification with the bull [Jake "The Bronx Bull" LaMotta [1941-54] of the Golden Age of Gloved Boxing, and "The Rock" AKA "The Brahma Bull" [circa 2000] of professional "wrestling" and cinema fame] is used successfully to project the image of a dominant boxer or pseudo-athlete.

All this symbology may simply be related to man's admiration for the contentious beasts that sired the herds upon which their wealth, mobility, and *nobility* was based. Perhaps herding people simply preferred more violent ritual combats than settled folk. However, maybe the rise of chariot warfare simply demanded a more lethal –more mobile—metaphor for combat than bloodless grappling.

Significantly the one ancient boxing culture which did not appear to embrace wrestling was the high palace culture of Crete [1700-1370 B.C.]. Among the elite of Crete bull-leaping was admired as a fine art and was engaged in by boys and girls. According to modern Spanish bull-fighters –a pretty fearless set—the practice appears suicidal. Bull-leaping may have been the basis for the legend of the Minotaur. Bull-fighting was also practiced by real Olympians, with the all-power-fighter Polydamas reportedly aping the heroes of myth by molesting a bull, as well as thumping that other much-abused animal of antiquity —the hapless Asiatic lion, hunted by naked egotistical jocks and armored megalomaniacal warrior-kings as well.

The fact that virtually all ancient boxing competitions were fought after an animal sacrifice or for a prize animal of great strength prefigures a long and disturbing trend of abusing some pretty helpless animals in order to advertise the prowess of a certain boxer—a brief survey should suffice:

19 B.C. The victor in boxing in Virgil's *Aeneid* crushes the skull of his prize bull to punctuate a boast.

A.D. 1951 Masutatsu Oyama, to prove the superiority of his karate, made two attempts to kill a bull with his bare hands at a slaughterhouse in the Japanese resort town of Tateyama. On his second attempt he knocked off a horn and scored a KO. Oyama's eventual bull-killing record was 36 horns & 3 kills in 52 tries.

Circa 1974, Roberto Duran KO'd a hapless horse with a single punch.

Whatever the reason -admiration of strength, sadism, or testicular envy—certain fighting men have, from the dawn of civilization, felt compelled to identify with and do violence to that venerable symbol of pastoral wealth and status, the bull.

Citizen

"A *coward*, --a man incapable either of defending or revenging himself, evidently wants one of the essential parts of the character of a man."
—Adam Smith *on the Wealth of Nations*

In ancient times, not only was bravery and martial prowess essential to manhood, they actually constituted manhood. A coward was destined to death or slavery, and could expect just such a fate. Not all societies place a high premium on one's individual autonomy. But, all societies place a high premium on their national autonomy. The idea of the nation has been in flux since the stone-age. In essence we are discussing man's attachment to his family. Over centuries of migration, settlement, growth, war and intermarriage the idea of one's nation expands from family, to clan, to tribe, to city, to region. In the present age our idea of nationhood is nearly continental, and some would say global. This expansive frame of reference does sometimes fragment into wars of ethnic cleansing and religious autonomy. However, the centuries-long trend seems to be one of expansion based on man's increasing ability to communicate and identify with his neighbors.

In regards to human social development and the rise of prize-fighting as a martial art form, the crucial stage is the advent of the city-state: a place to which one owed loyalty and life itself; behind the walls of which one's tribe gathered with neighboring tribes to form a defensible union against the barbarians of the hinterland; a place where it would no-longer be socially acceptable for a warrior to slay the warrior of another tribe in a duel, because this would result in a loss of manpower for the common defense. The development of the city state along these lines can be traced most clearly in Mesopotamia, Crete and Greece: the two first known prize-fighting centers and the land where prize-fighting became an international religion.

The man is of the city, and he must fight for the city, or his city and all whom he loves will die or be sold into slavery. Modern scholars have often stressed the cultural achievements of classical Greece, but the Greeks were genocidal to the core as the numerous genocides of the Athenians and Macedonians demonstrated. This is essentially a tribal mentality which requires a strong warrior ethic to maintain, a warrior ethic that must not descend into blood-feuds and daily mortal duels fought within the community.

For the citizens of such a belligerent city, striving for dominance in a warlike time, a ritual such as boxing, which promoted and even codified the virtues of courage, stamina and tenacity, while in close face-to-face contact with the opponent, was the perfect antidote to the type of endemic dueling that could result from multiple warlike tribes living in close proximity. Boxing also served as a reliable physical education tool that would help prepare the young men of the city for the stress of combat, without the jealous tribesman having to give over power to a robber king with his army of armed bullies.

As long as a city had enough men with the courage to fight, as displayed in the prize-ring, then regular practice at arms could at least produce a good militia force. Such militia forces were eventually defeated by the professional armies of empire-builders and [in Greece] were long terrorized by the professional army of Sparta, but they were adequate for their original purpose, which was contesting with one another over boundary disputes and fending off the barbarians from the Eurasian hinterlands.

Dancer

"He was a dancer whose every move cried danger."

—Roger Kahn, on Jack Dempsey, from *A Flame of Pure Fire*

War-dancing is something universal among tribal people though it seems to fade as civilization advances, until, in our present age, war and dancing are very rarely mentioned in the same breath. In classical Greece young men were expected to engage in gymnastic dances at coming-of-age ceremonies, and as a regular part of their training for military service. Armed dances, wrestling dances, dances that tell the story of a raid on farmers, and the shadow-fighting of boxers were all, in essence, dance activities.

In our own time the only dances that seem to fit this model of the dance preparing one for war would be the shadow-boxing of boxers, the forms, katas, hyungs, pormas and jurus of Chinese, Japanese, Korean, Filipino and Indonesian boxing arts, and solo weapon practice among fencers. Interestingly enough modern boxers value the music that thumps from their boom-boxes as a rhythmic tonic for their training, sometimes to odd extremes. Charles "Sonny" Liston, one of the most notorious fighters of the 20th Century, listened to the very same song, "Night Train", over and over again while in training.

It is also noteworthy that modern champions demand their own personalized entry music, with the best boxer of the late 1990s, Roy Jones Junior, even composing and recording his own music. The ancients used to gather to watch a prime boxer doing the shadow fight under the sun. Even Saint Paul had his opinion on shadow-boxing. Boeotia [Good-cattle-land], the prime grazing land of Greece, was also known as "The Dancing Floor of War", as so many battles were fought along its length of pasture.

A millennia and more before the athletic heyday of Classical Hellas [Greece is the Roman word for Hellas] two Babylonian freemen were depicted boxing to the accompaniment of a great drum beaten by two musicians. Throughout the Greco-Roman period Hellenic fist-fighters trained and battled to the music of flute and symbol. And their exploits were recorded in verse meant to be accompanied by the lyre [harp]. In the Roman period gladiators fought to the sound of a water-organ accompanied by various horns played by musicians seated as if for a modern orchestra arrangement. Plainly, dance among the ancients was seen as a fitting metaphor for war as well as good preparation for the individual martial artist. Just as instrumental music and marching songs were useful for close-order drill and served to relay battlefield commands, music was also seen as an appropriate accompaniment to the prize-fight.

Dance may somehow have been at the root of an ancient boxing tradition, though it should really be viewed as a supporting element. Just as the musician had his place in the military scheme, so he had a similar place in the world of athletics. The importance of musical accompaniment in ancient athletics and of the use of dance as a preparation is important to the course of our inquiry in that it points to an undeniable link between the military and athletic traditions of the ancient world.

Next to the duel, the boxing bout remains the most sanguine war-dance conceived by man, with the salient lesson that the true dance of life is meant to be a broken one. The boxer composes and improvises as an oddly joint effort with his antagonist, hoping that it shall be he, and not his opponent, who manages to write that final fateful verse.

Soldier

"I am a boxer again. I sense my opponent is reeling. I have lost three men since yesterday, but he has lost several times that many. That last outburst was a futile jab launched in anger and desperation, but essentially to cover a retreat. I can sense a knockout."

—James R. McDonough, *Platoon Leader*

A significant portion of the research done in support of *The Broken Dance* consisted of evaluating the military importance of boxing and related martial arts in the ancient Western world. This question will be addressed art-by-art and age-by-age, at-length and in detail throughout this study. At this point I would like to arm the reader with a modern analogy: the importance of modern amateur boxing to the modern counterpart of the ancient warrior; the combat infantryman...

It is obvious from the quote at the top of the page, as well as a few similar entries by James R. McDonough throughout his horribly enlightening memoir, that his experience as an amateur boxer helped him adapt mentally to the terror and confusion of the Vietnam conflict. There is obviously no room for the implementation of actual boxing methods on the modern killing fields [although, a friend of McDonough's –also a boxer—did kill a Vietcong with his bare fists before being killed when his firebase was overrun during a weapon lockdown]. But all four branches of the armed forces –the U.S. Navy in particular—do maintain competitive amateur boxing teams. Obviously there is a tradition of mental conditioning in the modern military that has changed little over the centuries; a tradition that values the fighting man's ability to stay cool under fire, whether it be the fire of slings, bows, muskets or A.K.-47s.

Since boyhood the author has had a fascination with infantry combat, and has read hundreds of war histories and interviewed dozens of combat infantrymen. The quality most admired by these fighting men and the authors of the various books was the ability to remain a functioning level-headed fighting man under the worst of circumstances. Upon coming under fire a fighting man who immediately rises up to attack often gives his comrades nothing but a corpse to account for. Likewise, the soldier who loses his nerve under fire is usually unable to join in the counterattack or even retreat in good order. What is required of the combat infantryman is mental balance under conditions of extreme dehumanizing violence; something most people cannot be brought to tolerate. Here is the parallel with boxing. Most people cannot be made to tolerate face punches.

One spring night in March of 2003 a Baltimore-area boxing coach trained two aspiring fighters: a 70 pound child, and a 200 pound high school football hero. He armed both fighters in gloves and head gear and directed the young man to defend against the punches of the child for 3 full minutes without hitting back or clinching. After 2 minutes under this pint-sized barrage of padded leather mittens the footballer screamed anxiously, tore off his head gear, and fled from the very same attack that a 12-year-old boy had withstood minutes before. Who would Sergeant York, Audie Murphy, Lewis Millet*, or James McDonough have wanted by their side? The cool-headed 12-year-old boy, or the 200-pound Friday-night warrior? Which type of fighter would you want passing the ammunition you needed to keep your position from being over-run by the enemy?

*Infantry heroes of WWI, WWII and the Korean Conflict respectively.

Sacrificial Slave to Criminal Entertainer

"Farewell, Patroklus, even there in Death's House!
All that I [Akhilles] promised once I have performed at last.
Here are twelve brave sons of the proud Trojans—
All, the fire that devours you takes them all..."
—Homer, *The Iliad*

The author must forever return to *Book 23* of *The Iliad*. It is in Homer's *Funeral Games for*

Patroklus that all the fertile seeds of ancient athletics rise from the ashes of human sacrifice. Boxing, the author firmly believes, was born as a blood sacrifice.

There is no more proof for this theory than the contention that boxing evolved as a form of fencing conditioning based on shield use. But the funerary influence on boxing is undeniable. The Olympics were essentially funerary games in honor of the hero-king Pelops. In the Roman era boxing maintained a closer association with gladiatorial combat than any other combat sport. There is, of course, clear evidence that Roman gladiatorial combats were first instituted as funeral offerings, following a similar Etruscan practice. The first boxing bout may very well have been fought by the light of a funeral pyre.

This all seems entirely gruesome to the modern mind. However, by permitting war-captives [slaves] to fight to the death in honor of the dead, the Romans were showing themselves to be far more civilized than Achilles—who comes off as something of a monster. Permitting half of their condemned slaves to live to be sacrificed another day was also practical. Boxing would be more practical yet; as it is sparing enough of life to be engaged in by socially valuable associates of the deceased. Conducted with the warriors' fencing hand gear without protective attire, such a ritual fist-fight insured the shedding of blood, even as the nature of the combat insured a passionate struggle, thus honoring the dearly departed who had lived and died under similar circumstances.

For the historian [inquirer] of ancient prize-fighting—which must encompass dueling— the warrior's funeral is the seed bed from whence all forms of ritual combat appear to spring. Of course, all of these: fencing [including stick-fighting]; wrestling; fist-fighting; and all-power-fighting, do have practical personal and military applications. These phenomena, that is, the ritual and practical application of personal combat, are not mutually exclusive. Even though the practical personal application of boxing may be physical fitness and the ability to defend one's self from confrontational assaults, and the military application is limited to psychological conditioning, all practitioners of the art, from fitness buff, to self-defense student, to combat infantryman, will measure their boxing ability and model their training according to the examples set by those celebrity boxers who practice their art in the most extreme ritualistic form—televised professional bouts. In addition, drawn from the lower "criminal" classes as they are, modern pro boxers recall the warrior-slaves of ancient Rome and the sacrificed warriors of earliest antiquity –fighters with limited options, struggling and bleeding to rekindle memories of the dead [past fighters] for onlookers who they do not necessarily represent –boxer like gladiator being both loved and despised by civil society.

Priest: Holy Men and Boxing from the Temples of Crete to Television Comedy

"Let us pray...
May it please my father I should offer him
These annual rites in his own shrine!
...I shall declare a race to be fought out
...Then boxing bouts for those who believe
In their skill with the gloves, come one and all!"
—Aeneas, from *The Aeneid* of Virgil

The core of preserved ancient boxing knowledge comes down to us courtesy of the various Greco-Roman priesthoods who promoted, sanctioned, refereed, judged and recorded the results of virtually all Greco-Roman boxing bouts. Priests set training standards at Olympia, commissioned wall-paintings praising slain boxers at Olympia and Nemea, and –most importantly—provided interviews for Pausanius [who leaves us with the most complete boxing records] concerning the fights of the classical champions. This all comes as no surprise. Priesthoods are the keepers of ritual. The boxing warriors of Babylon, Egypt and Crete are all depicted engaging in sacred rituals.

When compared to gladiatorial combat boxing can certainly be appreciated as a feminizing, violence-limiting ritual. The control of violence through strict combat rituals naturally falls to the priests –and in ancient Crete the priestesses—as the earthly authority on everything ritual. It may be that the ancient priesthood is more than a supporting factor in the development of boxing. Priestly sanction may be the basis for boxing, although I lack the evidence to support this hypothesis. Whatever the case for the involvement of ancient priests in the nurturing of prize-fighting, boxing and religion have maintained a unique and profound relationship for at least 3,800 years, as illustrated by some more recent points of interest:

1. 1200 A.D. Catholic Priest [Saint] Bernard of Sienna, Italy encouraged boxing as a substitute for [probably sword & buckler] dueling.
2. 1890s U.S. Navy Chaplain, Father William Reaney, promoted U.S. Navy boxing
3. 1970s The cast of the TV series M.A.S.H. included an actor portraying a boxing Chaplain

Beer-Drinker: Alcohol and Fisticuffs from Gimilninurta to Bobby Chyez

"Drinking beer,
in a blissful mood,
with joy in the heart and a happy liver."
—*Sumerian drinking song,* c. 2,500 B.C.

The association between alcohol and violence in our own time is well documented. Likewise the association of alcohol consumption with religious ritual among early civilizations is also well-documented. There does remain, however, the question of causality; did the consumption of alcohol amongst those civilizations who first instituted ritual fist-fighting cause –even in part—these violent rituals? This cannot be proved or disproved. But the instinct of the modern violence researcher and boxing coach merge easily into the suspicion that the fact that the ancient Mesopotamians were roaring drunks did something to encourage their support for boxing.

The curious story of Gimilninurta [found inscribed on a clay tablet unearthed at Sultan Tepe, Iraq, in the early 20th century] tells a tale that combines alcohol and fist-fighting...

Gimilninurta wanted to throw a party for friends and family, but had not the funds for the purchase of the all-important vats of beer that would be sipped with long reed straws to intensify the intoxication of his guests. Gimilninurta conceived of a scam whereby he would rent a borrowed goat to the mayor of Nippur in order to finance his party and then somehow avoid payment. Seeing through this blatant scheme the mayor had his servants beat the bearded player and toss him and his friend's goat into the street.

Bruised and disappointingly sober for the foreseeable future, Gimilninurta vowed revenge and swore to repay the mayor with three beatings. Posing as a doctor, a seer, and a burglar, Gimilninurta administered three beatings to the mayor, successfully solicited a loan from the king, got drunk, made a profit on the shindig, repaid the king with interest, and even commissioned a scribe to immortalize his story in baked clay!*

While researching this piece I happened upon a boxing magazine story concerning the alcohol-related legal problems of former middle-weight sensation Bobby Chyez. These two stories led me to reflect on the many stories of alcoholic fathers related by aspiring boxers; the fact that numerous modern gyms, prize-fighters and fight-promotion companies are managed by bar-owners who are often former fighters; that bar-owners buy many of the tables at amateur fight promotions; that local fight promotions and pay-per-view boxing events are often prominently advertised in bars where you can purchase tickets from the barmaid; and the fact that many of the dancers who work as ring card girls at these events are dating or related to boxers, who are sometimes working as bouncers at the very bars where these ladies are employed...

Alcohol use relates positively to ritual and violence. Boxing is a violent ritual often enjoyed by alcohol-imbibing spectators. Boxers are often drawn from the urban underclass where alcoholism is rampant. Since the bare-knuckle era professional boxers have looked toward the purchase and operation of a tavern as a means of investing their purses, with far more regularity and success than they have the foundation and operation of a boxing gym. The ritual of boxing certainly appears to be encouraged and nurtured by the use and misuse of alcohol.

*It is unclear why Gimilninurta's story was recorded and who sponsored the scribe who immortalized him.

Sailor

"The *skirmishes* [informal bouts] of our hero, while in the capacity of a sailor, are too numerous for recital…MILLING [boxing], it appears, formed the principal part of Scroggin's *amusement* when off duty."

—Pierce Egan, *Boxiana II*, 1818

From mythic sea captain Odysseus of the Odyssey, to legendary tough man and U.S. Navy veteran Tom Sharkey [1893-1904], to the current crop of U.S. Navy cadets fighting on the amateur boxing circuit out of Annapolis, Maryland, sailors have always had a reputation as tough scrappy prize-fighters that has gone hand-in-hand with their legendary appetite for alcohol and prostitutes. There are 3 obvious reasons for the boxing-sailor relationship: practicality; cross-cultural contact and discipline.

Limited space for shipboard sports while under sail remains the base case for supposing that the original boxers were sailors. The islands of eastern Hellas and the Greek colonies of Asia Minor and Sicily did provide the majority of top Greco-Roman boxers, not to mention the significance of the island of Crete to boxing history. It remains that sea traveling may have been the cause *and* conduit of ancient boxing. As for the practicality of boxing one must keep in mind the strong boxing tradition in the British Royal Navy which included bouts between drunken sailors who sat with their breeches tacked to their sea-chests, and ultimately produced bare-knuckle champion Tom King [1859-63], the nemesis of the great Jem Mace [1855-90]. The crowded conditions of ancient galleys and of the sailing ships of the bare-knuckle era would provide a logical framework for combat sport among their crews, which would naturally be encouraged by the presence of the wine ration among the Greeks and the rum ration among the British.

Although the causal evidence is very thin, the spread of prize-fighting appears to have been seaborne. British explorers in 1778 and 1805 reported on two different female boxing traditions among Polynesian islanders*. News of exciting activities spread quickly by sea in any era, and there was extensive contact between the bronze-age [2500 to 1000 B.C.] civilizations of Greece, Egypt, Crete and Phoenicia. Only the Phoenicians are not known to have had a boxing tradition, though they did facilitate contact between Mesopotamia and the Mediterranean islands and Greece.

Finally there is the question of the value of boxing as a disciplinary tool at the hands of the ship's captain. Whether as a means of settling disputes among men living in cramped quarters or as a form of aggression-venting sport, boxing obviously recommends itself to a captain in any age. Account must also be taken of the nature of the sailor, who obviously tends to be a risk-taker. Simply setting sail on the wide ocean in something smaller than an American row-home suggests an appetite for adventure not easily satisfied by common pastimes. As a final note, contestants at the sacred Hellenic festivals usually traveled by ship. They surely recruited some sparring partners in route.

*Islanders seem prone to prize-fighting. The natives of the Pacific Mortlock Islands were reported to have boxed with shark teeth enhanced hand gear. The inhabitants of Okinawa appear to have developed an independent boxing tradition before the introduction of Chinese forms. The Filipino and Indonesian islands are known to support a multitude of indigenous fighting forms. Finally, the natives of Rapa-Nui [Easter Island], Hawaii, and even the castaways on Pitcairn Island exhibited some extreme violent behavior that may be attributed to their geographic isolation.

Merchant: Assyrian Donkey Drovers in Anatolia to Cantonese Cooks in America

Life as a traveling merchant in the pre-modern world demanded the fighting ability to fend off criminals as well as the diplomatic ability to gain acceptance among a strange people in a distant land. Weapons, of course, were the means of defending against bandits, but frequent weapons prohibitions against foreigners in distant cities demanded that the merchant have some means of unarmed defense. For this purpose bodyguards, such as wrestlers, would certainly be employed.

It should here be noted that 19th and 20th Century Great Britain as well as early 20th Century America supported a number of carnivals where local tough-men would square off against the carnival wrestlers and boxers. The great Jimmy Wilde [130-3-1 with 99 KOs] began his career as a carnival fighter in Wales [circa 1908]. Former bare-knuckle champion "Gypsy" Jem Mace worked as a carnival fighter, as did American boxing author J.C. Thomas. The bare-knuckle boxing tradition has been kept alive primarily by the Travelers [English Gypsies] of Great Britain. When one notes that boxing has not always been acceptable, a link between traveling merchants and the art suggests itself.

In an earlier age when wrestling and boxing constituted sacred rituals it is not unreasonable to assume that certain merchants might have specialized in supplying kings and priests with fighters for their amusement. In fact, at least three Olympic boxers of ancient Greece traveled to the courts of Persian rulers to demonstrate their prowess. Later, in Roman times, there was a guild of traveling athletes based in Sardis, and also a brotherhood of traveling athletes based in Alexandria. The ability to travel securely in pre-modern times became an asset in and of itself. Professional level athletes of the Imperial age were notorious for traveling great distances for big purses.

There is also the link between sea-travel [the preferred means of travel for Greco-Roman athletes] and the merchant trade. Also the Babylonian culture from which we first gain a glimpse of men boxing was an aggressive cultural force across the entire ancient near east. Babylonian merchants and scribes ranged far and wide, making lucrative contacts, and serving as court advisors. From the donkey drovers of Assyria who traded in precious goods that they were often charged with keeping secret, to the Athenian businessmen who followed in the wake of Alexander's conquests, merchants were harbingers of cultural change, which would naturally include the most exciting public rituals of their parent culture.

The author once interviewed a high level karate master, who railed against Gung-fu as "the art of Chinese cooks", and associated the success of Chinese boxing clubs as being based on the fact that the attached eating establishment "paid the bills" as student enrollment couldn't. Stopping short of contrasting Chinese and Japanese boxing traditions, I must point out that these arts have been brought to America –and have eclipsed boxing as participation sports—by merchants more often than by prize-fighters.

Perhaps there was once a Babylonian barley-monger who owned a fist-fighting slave…

The Primal Logic of Prize-Fighting

Hunting is what our kind did for hundreds of thousands of years; so, to a certain extent –this author believes to a large extent—hunting is what we are, and what we will ever be, even if just hunters of knowledge.

It is the conclusion of this author that the man-to-man violence of war and sport is based on the man-to-animal violence of the hunt, and that boxing, therefore, is based ultimately on the hunt. The author's theory on the interconnection of hunting, warfare and sport is illuminated below.

Hunt-War-Sport

The hunt constitutes man's basis for his progressive interaction with the natural world and directly influences phenomena as diverse as nuclear war and sports photography, and constitutes the root cause for mankind's seemingly boundless and often trivial curiosity.

Mass Hunting is the practice of exterminating game animals in masse, such as driving a herd off a cliff or dropping dynamite into a fish pound. This behavior often reflects a people's lack of control over an environment and corresponding anxiety about surviving in that habitat, and is typical of new arrivals, such as the stone-age native Americans who wiped out the mega-fauna of prehistoric North America and the European settlers of colonial America who often wiped out the animal populations of entire regions to deny their aboriginal enemies a food source.

The man-to-man interaction that is based on mass hunting is commonly referred to as total war. However, one might also call this tribal or aboriginal war, as small populations without a strong economic base or sophisticated communications usually relied on the entire population to wage war; the elders planning, the men and older boys fighting, and the women maintaining and moving the base of operations. Such warfare witnesses much violence to women and children, and is often waged to exterminate competition for meager resources, with only enough enemy young adopted into the victorious tribe to replace losses.*

Subsistence Hunting is the trademark of the well-adapted hunter who hunts those members of the targeted prey population with the lowest reproductive value: the young; the old; the sick. Most animals hunt according to this logic as do primitives in marginal desert regions. Likewise, modern fisherman operating in ecologically threatened and heavily regulated estuaries, such as the Chesapeake Bay, must abide by exacting standards to insure the health of the prey population.

The man-to-man corollary to subsistence hunting would be raiding, banditry and piracy. This type of behavior is rarely engaged in by modern nations and is now the province of criminal organizations. [Most modern nations have acquired through law all the rights that the criminal acquires through force.] Warfare between peoples in any age that corresponds to the subsistence hunting model is liable to be constant and of a low intensity, with occasional flare ups of the mass hunting impulse in periods of crisis. The American frontier of the Old North West during the revolutionary war period was a good example of such a military situation, as are some modern insurgencies.

Trophy Hunting is most often engaged in by high status individuals of early civilizations and by primitives seeking high status among their fellows. It consists almost exclusively of hunting very dangerous game–preferably male predators—or of large male representatives of a prey population which possess appealing headgear to be taken as trophy racks. Societies which engage in this type of hunting are often on the cusp of ecological domination. There is also a tendency toward a class-based right to hunt, favoring the aristocracy at the expense of the mass of servile peasants, who are often simply the survivors of a farm-based population that has been conquered by a hunting-herding people. Bull-fighting is a direct modern descendent of the trophy hunts of ancient kings and primal big-men, as is the "buck" phase of whitetail deer season in the Eastern United States.

The man-to-man behavior that is based on trophy hunting is clearly the duel. In fact, the concept of the trophy hunt or duel may be expanded until a mass battle is conceived of as a duel between peoples. This model of combat results in what has come to be known as limited war, waged according to certain rules and customs, while preserving the resources over which the combatants are fighting for control.

Submission Hunting is the act of capturing and releasing or capturing and domesticating prey. Some forms of modern sport-fishing and photography are direct descendents of this practice, as is rodeo competition. The practice of submission hunting demonstrates a high level of human control over the environment and may actually result in its alteration. Another side-effect of this practice is the development of mass herding techniques which are easily generalized for use in war. Hence the nomadic conquerors of the ancient world [Indo-Europeans and Huns], periodically emerging from the Eurasian hinterlands, were all but unstoppable in their time.

The man-to-man corollary to submission hunting is the unarmed prize-fight. Virtually all pre-modern forms of boxing were submission arts as was, and is, MMA. Even upright grappling forms which aim for a throw rather than a submission or choke are essentially submission arts, as the throw to the back is symbolic of the submission of the downed prey animal [look at rodeo steer-roping] and of the human female.

There can be little doubt that hunting provides the basis for warfare, dueling and prize-fighting. The weapons of the warrior and the hunter were originally identical, as were the submission techniques of the prize-fighter and the hunter:

throwing, choking and [cow] punching. Indeed those ancient heroes most revered by the ancients, Gilgamesh and Herakles, were renowned as hunters, warriors, and prize-fighters. It has also been the practice throughout history among certain flamboyant boxers aspiring to greatness to abuse domestic cattle with their fists. There is an undeniable link between animal fighting and prize-fighting in the ancient and modern worlds.

*Utely, *The Lance and the Shield,* pages 14-25

Figure 4.
The First Warriors
Mesolithic cave painting, Morela la Vella, Spain, c. 20,000 B.C.

This is the first known depiction of men fighting. Note: the symmetry of arms [all seven warriors are archers]; the close proximity of combat; and the dominance of the central figure, who is the object of attention for the three enemy warriors, who have consequently been outflanked by his three comrades. Is it a coincidence that the first known picture of men fighting depicts a symmetrical conflict and a dominant risk-taker [hero]? Or does this picture simply state the universal desire of warriors for the best weapons available [the bow was a relatively recent invention, providing the best available fire-power] and to be led by example rather than be managed from the rear? Interestingly enough the first known depiction of men wrestling was painted in a cave a mere hundreds of miles away in the south of France, some 4,000 years later.

The Personal Appeal of Boxing

"When I was matched against this older Italian fighter who was fifty and ten—a real tough guy—he looked across the ring at me and said, 'Kid, I'm gonna feed your mother your head!' When I got out there and hit him he was like a rock! I had twenty KOs but I knew this guy wasn't going down. I could feel it in my bones. So I boxed..... I felt safe –stepped into this special place that always elevated me above the opponent when I won by decision..."

—"Irish" Johnny Coiley, interview with the author, 1989

Thus far our inquiry into the origins of boxing has focused on social elements that may have facilitated the birth and growth of the art. At this point the reader is asked to shift his attention from the life-way or station-in-life of the boxer to the purely personal perspective of the private individual who takes up the practice of boxing. What exactly is the purely personal, selfish appeal of boxing? What is the aspect of boxing that keeps boxers going beyond any hope of fame or fortune? Is this appeal intellectual, emotional, esoteric or animalistic?

At this point our inquiry takes a murky turn into the psychology of the martial artist. Former Heavyweight Champion George Foreman once said, 'Boxing is the sport to which all other athletes aspire.' Why do some ball-players gaze with envy at the boxer? Why also, as the author has witnessed and experienced on so many occasions, is boxing the art that so intrigues, menaces and revolts practitioners of Asian-based martial arts?

Although boxing coaches and boxing writers rarely mention Asian-based martial arts, karate and kung-fu instructors and commentators are forever making analogies to boxing. Discussions about how to beat a boxer in a "street-fight" through the use of karate and other Asian arts have been regular fare in martial arts journals since the 1970s. Likewise, sportswriters and ballplayers toy with the idea of a dominant ball-player crossing over to the prize-ring and challenging the current heavyweight champion: NBA all-star Wilt Chamberlain was put forward as a probable opponent for Muhammad Ali; NFL prospect Tony Mandrich was touted as the nemesis of Mike Tyson; and NFL all-stars Ed "Too Tall" Jones and Mark Gastenau waged dreadfully lackluster boxing campaigns. However, during this same time-frame [1970s, 80s & 90s] not a single pro boxer attempted such a move, nor was there any such calls from the press.*

Boxing has something that almost everybody wants, but that almost nobody will take the risk of actually boxing to attain. In early 21st Century America pro boxers are regarded as odd folks around whom myths seem to coalesce. Even unremarkable amateur boxers are viewed by their everyday acquaintances and martial arts colleagues as people who have somehow been touched by an otherworldly force. To better understand how the practice of boxing as a low-level competitor or simple gym-fighter can effect one's life, and help keep fascination about the art alive, consider the following anecdotes involving some ordinary amateur boxers...

A slow-fisted boxer was helping two supermarket clerks finish up a honey display a minute before quitting-time when a 2-pound jar fell off the top shelf. As the two clerks stared dejectedly at the plunging jar –which would mean working over for free and missing their bus as they cleaned the spill—the boxer instinctively snatched the jar as it reached shoulder-height. From that point on the clerks developed a palpable dread for the boxer as if he were a voodoo-using assassin.

A mediocre amateur middleweight was invited to spar a heavyweight karate instructor who he easily KO'd. The middleweight is now regarded as a fistic wizard by the local karate community.

A boxing pool-player was standing aside for a game when a cue-ball popped up and spun toward the pretty face of the only female patron in the bar – whom all the players were attempting to impress. After snatching the ball from in front of the girl's face the oft-defeated boxer was not permitted to pay for his drinks, as the patrons equated his superior eye-hand coordination with his many boxing victories.

A welterweight boxer, who was unfairly accosted by a 300lb bouncer in a seedy nightclub, KO'd the bouncer and was permitted to leave the nightclub unmolested by the supervising bouncer.

A lightweight boxer who worked as a technician in a hospital emergency room KO'd a large male intruder with a jab and returned to his duties.

A high school football coach/gym teacher invited the stars of his varsity football team to play a game of "head-shot" dodge-ball, with volley balls, against some freshmen students who did not want to play on the football team. Throughout the one-sided slaughter one of the freshman, a boxer, used his ability to slip punches to avoid the head shots thrown by the football players.

The accounts of small amateur boxers knocking out large attackers are legion, and to a large extent probably account for the mystical awe attached to the practice of boxing. Of course, the sensible practice of Asian-based self-defense arts can also produce an unusual ability to incapacitate aggressors, so there must be something more to the appeal of boxing than the shadow of the knockout.

As a boxing and stick-fighting coach who has trained with many types of martial artists, the author can list with conviction three aspects of the boxer's art that most seem to intrigue practitioners of other arts, and set the boxer in a special niche that these practitioners love to visit but dread the thought of remaining in:

1. *Empathy.* Due to the high-level of one-to-one, face-to-face, arms-length contact, the experienced boxer cultivates the ability to "read" his opponent, to sense the opponent's anxiety.
2. *Austerity.* As an art-form that focuses on training or conditioning rather than on "practice" and "learning". Boxing offers the experienced boxer an uncanny calm and grace under pressure that most intrigues and frightens those fighters who have spent their time attempting to learn "skills". The boxer develops a degree of conditioning that permits him to behave naturally in unnatural circumstances.
3. *Naked Power.* Boxing is a naked art, and the raw ability to stretch a man senseless without a weapon, and without the gross anxiety of a protracted struggle, makes the boxer an intriguing figure, dispensing as he does

virtual death without much visible stress or the intrusion of a weapon.

As our inquiry proceeds the reader will be treated to a virtual feast of *empathy, austerity* and *naked power*, as appreciated by those ancient societies who placed such a premium on these prize-fighting attributes that their passion for boxing remains with us to this day.

*Roy Jones Junior did play minor-league basketball out of sheer boredom in the 1990s. But this hardly constituted an attempt to challenge the primacy of NBA all-star and front-man Michael Jordan.

Ritual Combat

"Aruru, you created this man,
So now create a rival for him
To equal his spirit and discipline.
Let them be ever in conflict, so that Uruk may know
Peace and quiet."
-The Epic of Gilgamesh

Ritual combat is a method of managing violence within a group or between kin groups. Many parallels between humans and animals may be drawn to illustrate the uses of ritual behavior to moderate violence within a group. While ungulates, such as deer, possess antlers for use in ritual combat with rivals of their own species, they will defend against predators with their more deadly hooves. Likewise men learned how to limit force through various ritual forms of combat. In periods when warfare is symmetrical and heavily ritualized, like 18th Century Europe and Classical Greece, combat sports tend to proliferate.

The first condition for the practice of ritual combat is respect of, and empathy for, one's adversary. This is a universal precondition for fighting according to artificial rules. The desire to be respected by the enemy is equaled by the desire to engage a respected enemy of appropriate status. These dual needs are best attested by the lengthy, and genealogical, introductions shouted by the heroes of the Iliad, and the adoption of coats- of-arms by medieval knights. This empathy, respect and cultural identification is further enhanced by the practice of fighting according to commonly held customs. Engagement in these rituals insures the warrior status in life and death.

Ritual Victory

"Rivalry is a densely textured relationship, building opposition out of similarity, and solidarity out of the intimacy of shared ambition and mutual envy...there were no equals, and no second chances."

-Inga Glendinnen, Aztecs, an Interpretation

Victory conditions for mutual combat evolve from death, to incapacitation, to submission, to first blood and other technical points. To thrive as a spectator sport a combat ritual must constitute a dangerous and exhausting trial, with victory conditions that are grossly visual, such as: throws, pins, submissions, knockdowns, knockouts and visible damage to the combatant. The knockout is the king of victory conditions, the submission is queen.

Most forms of ritual weapon combat either become extinct as soon as they are no longer relevant to battlefield conditions, or fade into non-lethal obscurity as soon as the social conditions that enabled that form of dueling change. An example of the former case would be the extinction of the gladiatorial arts at the end of the Roman period, as the importance of close-quarter infantry combat was losing relevance on the battlefield in the face of the barbarian horse armies from the east. More typical of the fate of dueling traditions would be the degeneration of the long sword arts of Japan and Europe: ultimately resulting in the sports of kendo and foil fencing. These two sports are, in essence, games that do not have the purpose of producing adaptable weapon-fighters, as they utilize mock training weapons as opposed to modified dueling arms, and prohibit strikes to targets favored by actual duelists, such as leg and wrist slashes and thrusts to the face.

Combat sports that reward only technical points, and fail to reward the use of incapacitating force, do not maintain their appeal. Olympic boxing is the best example of this fact. Combat sports, such as karate, that reward only technical points, and actually penalize the use of force, have no spectator appeal, and are on the road to extinction as fighting arts.

While all weapon arts have become extinct or have devolved into dance, meditation or gamesmanship, some unarmed forms of ritual combat have continued to reemerge as popular spectacles throughout history, and have managed to remain relevant to contemporary military establishments. For a form of ritual combat to maintain its cultural status it must be demonstrated as a public spectacle, the focus of which is to incapacitate or submit the opponent.

Chapter 7
Of Perfect Might: Ritual Combat in Ancient Mesopotamia—2600 to 1000 B.C

"The great gods made Gilgamesh perfect in form:
...Two-parts god and one-part man.
His body had the strength of a wild bull:
Nothing could withstand the might of his weapons
And his subjects would wake to the beating of his drum."

—*The Epic of Gilgamesh*

The ancient ideal of the flawed yet potent hero–physically perfect but ambitiously overreaching—still finds expression in the modern world. The sagas of the ancient heroes echo most brutally in the modern prize-ring. Likewise, at the dawn of civilization, young men competed for heroic status in wrestling bouts and boxing matches. Unlike the modern prize-fighter, who engages in an ancient vestigial ritual, the ancient prize-fighter imitated the current geopolitical reality; as his head-of-state was expected to answer the challenge to duel from any rival king. The question that remains unanswered about the ancient prize-fighter is his motivation: was he imitating the king; identifying with the king; preparing to become the king; or was he the king?

Everyday Life in the Garden of Eden

If ever there was a state of servitude accepted as righteous by the servile class it would have been the lot of the ditch-diggers of Mesopotamia. They had to devote themselves en masse to the cooperative efforts of irrigation and cultivation in the semi-desert of ancient Iraq. This naturally required a level of centralized organization that rendered these folk easily manipulated. In addition, the narrowly defined and strenuous nature of their task had taken them so far from their hunting life-way that they became unfit for war and hence easy prey for the hunter-nomads of the hinterlands.

To avoid extermination, the best such men could hope for was to become the willing slaves to the chief of such a nomad tribe; or similarly submit to the whims of a home-grown cast of war-fighters. Imagine a world run by organized crime; life as one big protection racket. The remedies developed to soothe the symptoms of this terminal social state formed the very foundations of civilization. The grinding labor and low-protein diet of the farmer made life weak, short and miserable. However, he would rarely starve outright and lived life in a state of near perpetual drunkenness. He had no individual freedoms but he could enjoy his beer and the company of a state-sponsored prostitute.

Though his wife would age quickly, his sons would serve a better man, his daughters would become the property of brutes, and he would surely not understand the unseen forces that would drag him riddled with pain from his wretched life; he would not suffer murder, starvation or torture. For any poor soul unlucky enough to have been born a farmer in ancient Iraq slavery really was the ancient equivalent to life at an all-inclusive resort. Welcome to the world of the first boxers.

Map 2 (next page)
The Rise of Ritual Combat in Ancient Mesopotamia to 1000 B.C.

Known among historians as "The Fertile Crescent" and "The Cradle of Civilization", The Land Between the Rivers was apparently the first region of the world to witness large scale military conflict and state-sponsored ritual combat. This map indicates the location and date-of-origin of artifacts associated with ritual combat.

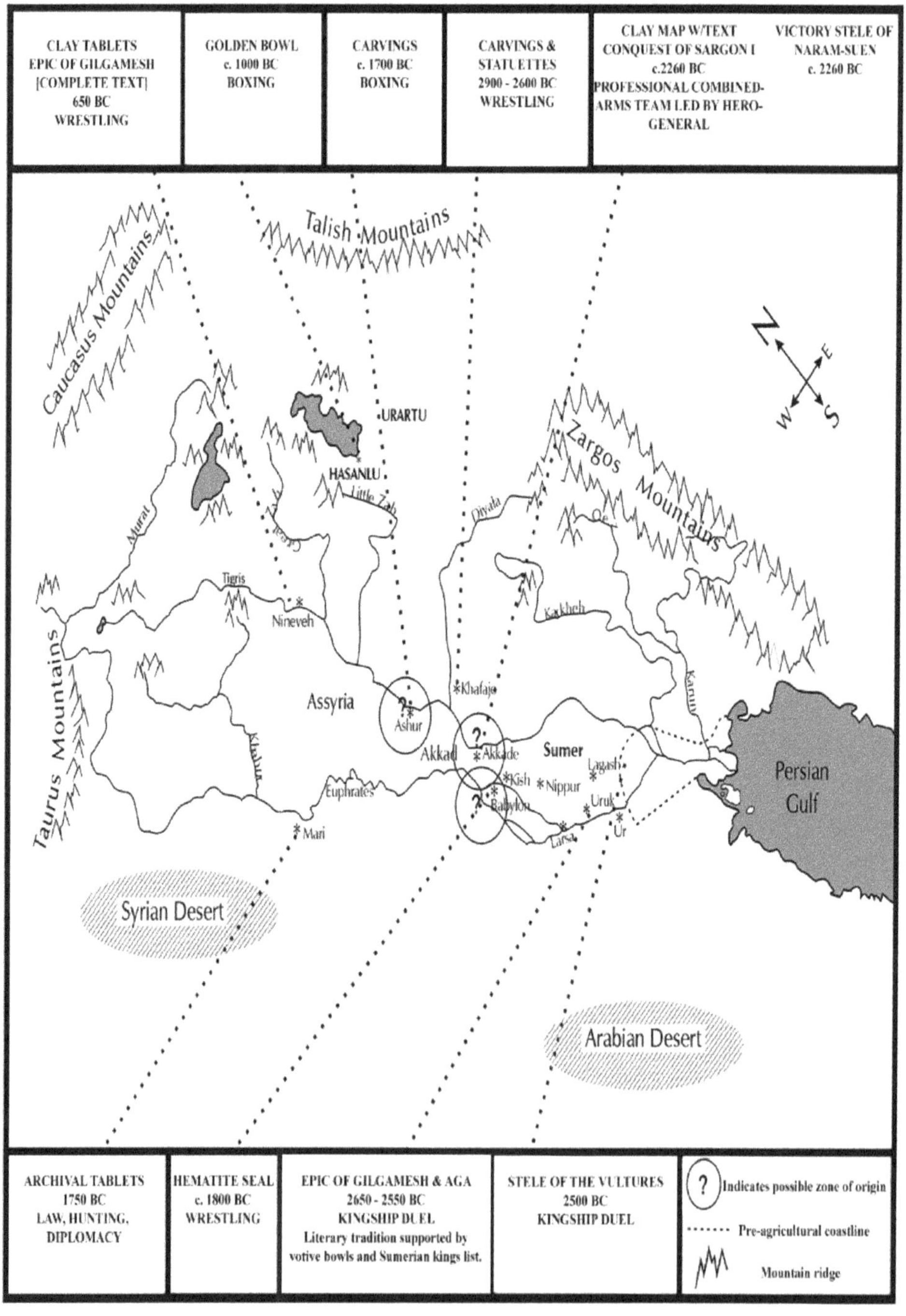
CLAY TABLETS
EPIC OF GILGAMESH
[COMPLETE TEXT]
650 BC
WRESTLING
GOLDEN BOWL
c. 1000 BC
BOXING
CARVINGS
c. 1700 BC
BOXING
CARVINGS &
STATUETTES
2900 - 2600 BC
WRESTLING
CLAY MAP W/TEXT
CONQUEST OF SARGON I
c.2260 BC
PROFESSIONAL COMBINED-ARMS TEAM LED BY HERO-GENERAL
VICTORY STELE OF
NARAM-SUEN
c. 2260 BC
Talish Mountains
Caucasus Mountains
URARTU
HASANLU
Little Zab
Zargos Mountains
Diyala
Murat
Tigris
Nineveh
Taurus Mountains
Assyria
Ashur
Khafaje
Akkad
Akkade
Sumer
Kish
Nippur
Lagash
Babylon
Uruk
Larsa
Ur
Euphrates
Mari
Karun
Persian Gulf
Syrian Desert
Arabian Desert
N
E
W
S
ARCHIVAL TABLETS
1750 BC
LAW, HUNTING,
DIPLOMACY
HEMATITE SEAL
c. 1800 BC
WRESTLING
EPIC OF GILGAMESH & AGA
2650 - 2550 BC
KINGSHIP DUEL
Literary tradition supported by votive bowls and Sumerian kings list.
STELE OF THE VULTURES
2500 BC
KINGSHIP DUEL
? Indicates possible zone of origin
Pre-agricultural coastline
Mountain ridge

Sacred Hands: The Plight of a Temple Wrestler c. 2600 B.C.

Gust had worked his entire life for this day on the top platform of the Holy Stair. His family had worked as well: his father and brothers toiling into the night so that he would be free to train; his mother serving the priests for scraps of meat to feed his aspirations; his sisters had lain with the slayers and merchants to acquire his oil and chalk.

Ten years past, as a young bull of 16 years, he had been permitted to join the wrestlers at the temple gate and wait for the honor to clinch-up with Red Lion, First Wrestler of Canal City, bodyguard of the Priest King. For ten years he had not missed a day at the gate; the first to arrive and last to leave. All sweltered at the gate and clinched-up with one-another for the right to clinch-up with Red Lion when he came down from the temple for his evening training. For the past 3 years no other wrestler than Gust ever awaited Red Lion when the shadow cast by the Holy Stair banished the sun from the gateway.

Red Lion was being put out to pasture. He was huge, awesome and strong. But Gust had been taking it easy on him for these past 6 moons. The man had grown old and slow, fat around his middle. He was the Priest King's companion though, and would enjoy an easy retirement. Gust's family waited outside the gate with him on this day, household goods in hand, ready to move into their new apartments among the menial staff.

The Priest of the East Gate and an armored slayer escorted Gust up the Holy Stair, where Red Lion waited with the Priest King; a man tall, gaunt, fierce, and maimed by war. Gust had seen him often, and had avoided starring at the missing ear, half-hand and empty eye-socket. He was their master, and they were right to fear him.

Having ascended the platform Gust stood in silence, awaiting his command, as the priest and slayer descended the stair and left him alone with the most feared man in The Land Between the Rivers, and his household protector. The Priest King spoke in a voice harsh and accustomed to command, "Gust, before you clinch-up with my old bull here I want you to understand, that defeating him will do him no harm. I brought some sleek fat whores back for him from up-river. He'll have it easy in his old age...

Your life though, will be hard. You will guard me and snap the necks of those who oppose or undermine me. I will die long before you. You will strangle my favorite wives in my funeral cart, and then have to survive by your wits when my sons come to blows over the inheritance. Yours will not be a long life laying with sleek women and drinking beer. You will live a terribly interesting life. Do you accept such a life Gust?"

"Yes protector. You are Top Man and protect all, so I swear to protect and serve you."

Gust was feeling pleased with his answer when a roar brought him to his senses, and he realized, with the barest instant to spare, that Red

Lion, charging him like a bull, was determined to make him pay for his new honors.

Their foreheads smashed together and blood flowed as their chests collided with a great smack. The clinch-up soon came, and Red Lion was reaching around for Gust's belt, intent on throwing him down the Holy Stair. Gust remained confident though; the man was already losing his patience—the leg-lock came surely and more easily than he could have hoped for. As he slid into position on the hard-baked bricks and broke the big man's ankle, he wondered, *is this how it will end for me?*

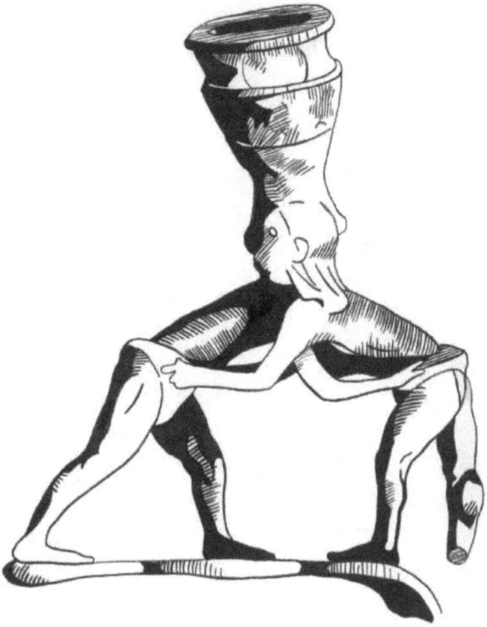

Figure 5.
Sumerian Belt Wrestlers
Bronze Statuette, Khafaje, Iraq, c. 2900 to 2600 B.C.

Belt wrestling is the unarmed martial art form that is most compatible with the primary martial art of the ancient world, which is fencing [the practice of fighting with muscle-powered weapons]. Military fencing in particular places great emphasis on remaining standing during combat, regarding any downed fighter as a casualty, as he is liable to be trampled and crushed in the press of battle. The art form depicted by these joint figurines [which constituted a base for twin vases] is echoed in the modern Japanese art of *sumo*, which might possibly represent the world's oldest continuous surviving martial tradition.

Figure 6.
Sumerian Wrestlers
Relief carving, Khafaje, Iraq, c. 2900 to 2600 B.C.

From right to left these three pairs of belted wrestlers engage in tactics that go beyond [and most likely predated] the push and tug of belt wrestling:

Right. Sparring for position [the phase of ancient freestyle wrestling that probably inspired boxing].

Center. Attacking the base [attempting to throw] with a double-grasp and trip.

Left. Attempted ankle lock, indicating a submission art form, opposed to a simple throwing contest.

The Kingship Duel

"Gilgamesh led out his arms against Kishi,
captured the bodies of its seven heroes,
and stomped on lord Agga's head as on [the head of] a snake."

—*Gilgamesh and Agga*

The warlords of Sumer led bodies of massed spearmen into combat, but they, themselves, and their select heroes [personal retainers, probably warrior-slaves], fought as individuals in the no-man's-land between the opposing armies. These duels were matters of martial pride affecting the entire community, and were subject to strict etiquette. In fact, such duels were sometimes instigated by written invitations which even stipulated the color of the cloths to be worn by the dueling kings! Enmerkar, king of Uruk, was challenged to a duel by the king of Aratta, in which the specific color and pattern of the attire was stipulated. It should be noted that modern bare-knuckle and gloved boxing bouts have usually been occasions for the display of personal, political, ethnic, or team colors. Any reading of a modern boxing equipment catalog will drive this point home.

As indicated by the *Steele of Vultures*, from Telloh, dated 2500 B.C., depicting king Eannat of Lagash wielding his short sword at the head of a mass of spearmen, these leaders valued personal combat at close range to the point of deriving their actual political identity from this practice. A practice for which boxing –of the type depicted in the *Hero-Duel of the Boxers* [see Figure 7.] would have been excellent sub-lethal preparation.

The physical primacy of early kings set the standard for the athletes of the Greco-Roman world: kings fought alone against their equals; were the only hunter permitted to kill lions*; and required the personal man-to-man loyalty of expert retainers [corner-men, so to speak].

The symbolic and practical action of the hero-king leading his army at the head of a select body of retainers remained crucial to warfare from the dawn of civilization to at least the time of Alexander the Great. It is no accident that after the death of the last great hero-king [Alexander**] in 323 B.C. and the indiscriminate rampaging of his war-machine, that various cults dedicated to the supreme individual combatant emerge: the *Olympic* "Successors" of Herakles [272 B.C.]; Roman *gladiatorial* rites [264 B.C.]; backing of a boxing contender [Aristonikus] by a transnational tyrant [The King of Ptolemaic Egypt] for the 142nd *Olympiad* [212 B.C.]; and the rise of international prize-fighting *synods* and the cult of the *periodonikes*[100s B.C.]

**Mari Archives*

Yakkim Adad, Mayor of Akkaka, wrote to his king concerning a marauding lion which he did not have the authority to kill. There is also an indication in this collection that dogs, bears and boars were used to guard city gates, which would make dangerous animals military assets jealously guarded by the feuding kings.

**It may be argued that Philopoemen of Akhaea and Hannibal Barca of Carthage were hero-kings. However, neither was a sovereign tyrant, but rather a patriotic hero/general.

Seven, the Number of the Hero

"...And Enkidu took her.
She did not recoil, but tempted him...
...she taught the wild-man the woman's art
And he was attracted to her and joined with her.
For six days and seven nights Enkidu coupled with the whore."

—*The Epic of Gilgamesh*

After being tamed by the woman Enkidu becomes destined to rival and then serve Gilgamesh, who, like all heroic tyrants since, could not cut a heroic figure without lesser heroes to illuminate his deeds. Without Joe Frazier and George Foreman we wouldn't have had such a great Muhammad Ali. Likewise, without Enkidu, the Epic of Gilgamesh would have been just another bronze-age boast inserted into a pedestrian kings list by a paid hack.

Such movies as *Tears of the Sun, Dog Soldiers, Predator, The Magnificent Seven, The Expendables,* and *Seven Samurai* are built around the ancient idea of seven doomed heroes. Older tales such as J.R.R. Tolkien's *Lord of the Rings*, Aeschylus' *Seven Against Thebes* and various creation and flood stories imbedded in near eastern myth point to the depth of this tradition.*

The seven heroes of myth may simply be built around the idea of seven sacred days which derives from the seven visible moving heavenly bodies, forming the basis for the week as a division of the lunar month. There is also the question of the relation of the number seven to geographic and city-planning records: the seven mountains and demons of the early Sumerian Epics**; the Seven Seas [that even made it onto the modern dinner table in the form of salad dressing]; Seven-gated Thebes; and The Seven Hills of Rome...

Whatever the origin of the seven heroes the number seven remained significant to the ritual combatants of Classical Greece and Imperial Rome, as heroes and kings continued to treasure shields covered with seven layers of tough bull's hide, and boxers as late as 400 A.D. wrapped their knuckles in seven layers of bull's hide. Furthermore, the ultimate boast of a single event winner at Olympia was to prevail over seven opponents without a bye. [An unmatched competitor who sits out a round or heat has taken a "bye".]

*Hooke, S. H. *Middle Eastern Mythology*, Penguin, NY, 1963, pages 11-57, 149-55

**Kramer, Samuel Noah. *From the Tablets of Sumer: Twenty-Five Firsts in Man's Recorded History*, Falcon Wing, Indian Hills, Colorado, 1964, pages 202-19

The Hero in the Machine

"Yet for all this emphasis on the emerging power of groups and organizations, it is important to remember that war is still based on the life and death of the individual."

—Robert L. O'Connell, *Of Arms and Men*

The hero is uniquely popular in ancient and modern literature, and according to the work of many 19th and 20th Century anthropologists he is the stuff of stories for pre-literate people as well. If we are to understand the fact and function of the ancient boxer and his art we must keep in mind that he represents the hero, and not just any hero, but the kind of hero that members of a mass society or "civilization", can readily identify with.

The boxer—as does any prize-fighter—contends according to a set of rules which tend to be both cruel to the participant and frustrating to his efforts. This represents the lot of everyone in an ancient society where even kings and queens lived lives that would be considered harsh by modern standards.

The art of the boxer is pursued more frequently as the scope of war becomes more dehumanizing. In small scale hunting societies facing constant opportunities for heroics there is no need for the ritual of boxing. In early civilizations where the petty tyrant can wield power with the aid of anywhere from seven to a hundred picked men, boxing rises as a useful ritual; as part of a war-fighter's training regime and as a communal entertainment.

However, boxing usually becomes wildly popular at those times in man's history when developments in warfare have marginalized the role of the individual combatant to the point of obscurity. The first known boxing tradition developed in Babylon just as the composite bow made warfare less personal and more lethal. The great age of Olympic boxing in Classical Greece – which witnessed 6 of the 11 best ancient boxers—coincided with the rise of hoplite warfare. The development and unleashing of the Macedonian and Roman war machines influenced all forms of prize-fighting profoundly from wrestling to dueling. Boxing emerged again in Europe with the rise of gunpowder warfare and its popularity intensified with each order of magnitude advance in the art of killing with firearms. The bare-knuckle boxing craze of Regency England coincided with the Napoleonic Wars. The American Civil War coincided with the rise of bare-knuckle boxing in America. And, at last, the period spanning the Great World Wars of the 20th Century marked the Golden Age of modern gloved boxing. In the interval between these two spasms of mass killing the fascist tyrants Hitler and Mussolini even used boxing [as well as innocent boxers Max Schmeling and Primo Carnera] as propaganda tools. During WWII the U.S. Military actively courted boxers as public relations men and morale boosters.

These military-related boxing trends indicate a popular need to reaffirm the image of the warrior as the hot-blooded champion of pre-historic tradition against the image of the cold-blooded killer dispensing death as part of an efficient war-machine. For us this may be a function of a collective subconscious. But for the Babylonians this may have reflected a conscious effort not to forget the personal risks assumed by their nomadic grandfathers. Boxing is a kind of martial nostalgia sporadically enjoyed on a mass scale.

Figure 7.
Hero-Duel of the Boxers

Reconstruction of Babylonian relief carving, based on a written description of the musicians by Karen Rhea Nemet-Jejat, and a relief carving of two boxers from Ashunnak, Mesopotamia [held at the Louvre Museum] Central Mesopotamia [Akkad] c. 1700 B.C.

The boxers in this depiction are fully clothed and are sporting the traditional headgear of the Babylonian elite. [Were they slaves, this would be apparent by their hairstyle.] The clothing and the wrist band [more suited for fencing than boxing] suggest the possibility of martial exercises practiced in a mixed format, or engagement in a young boxing tradition recently divorced from a fencing context.

The large drum in the background would be an Akkadian* *lilissu*-drum which played an important part in masculine Akkadian rituals. One must not rule out the possibility of boxing as a funerary right based on the presence of the drum, which, along with the *mikku* [drum-stick] constituted a magical device associated with the realm of the dead or underworld.**

The boxing technique is conservative and primitive keeping with the bare-knuckle tradition of vertical fist alignment and a low guard. The cocking of the elbow of the rear hand just above and behind the hip indicates a primitive understanding of power punching mechanics, which, coupled with the flat-footed postures, is reminiscent of modern karate.

The crucial question concerning the boxers depicted in this piece is whether they are meant to be stylized mirror images or actual individual combatants? This author is of the opinion that this constitutes a depiction of two specific individuals, and accordingly, offers the following analysis: The larger [right-handed] fighter in the foreground to the left is dominating the combat from a central position, as the smaller boxer to the right attempts to outmaneuver the larger fighter by stepping around to his right behind his right lead [he is either left-handed or has adopted the southpaw style out of necessity], firing a right jab which the big man shields against with a simple high lead guard.

Note: The lead elbow of the smaller fighter is much farther removed from his body than the elbow of his opponent, indicating that he is jabbing, and that the opponent is guarding. The flat-footed posture and chambered rear hand indicate a style of boxing analogous to shield and spear fighting; guarding with the lead hand and thrusting with the rear hand, with distracting, covering, and harassing blows delivered with the lead "shield" hand.

*The pre-Babylonian conquerors of Sumer who may have introduced boxing.

**Hooke, *Middle Eastern Mythology*, pages 55-56

Figure 8.
Gilgamesh and Enkidu

Based on a hematite seal, held in the Yale Babylonian collection, central Mesopotamia, c.1800 B.C.

The human hero Gilgamesh is depicted to the left, probably wrestling the Bull of Heaven.

His companion Enkidu, is represented as a bull-man to the right, and is depicted wrestling with a monster, probably the demon Humbaba.

Both combatants wear belts but tie-up the limbs, suggesting that the wrestling art that was current during the composition of this seal was one supplementary to a rough form of military fencing. Mechanics aside, the metaphor here is simple; men of power are belted [representing their armed status] and they dominate the simple beasts and monsters that once terrified less potent men.

Figure 9.
Dragon Boxer

Reconstruction of a scene from the Golden Bowl of Hasanlu, based on a written description by M.G.P. Insley, a degraded photocopy of a photograph of the artifact, an untitled archaeological report, and an online illustration of a portion of the bowl. Hasanlu, Urarturia [Armenia/Iran], c.1000 B.C.

Artifact Notes: The bowl was excavated in 1959, is 21cm high, 25cm wide, is partially crushed on one end, weighs 950 grams, and is housed at the Iranian National Museum.

Context: The boxing scene is depicted in the bottom register below a sky-god mounting a chariot, pulled by an oxen, which is devouring [or exhaling] the tail of the three-headed beast that forms the back portion of the "dragon" or "chariot of the sky-giant", against which the hero boxes. Behind the hero are two scenes of sacrifice or worship depicting a man similar in appearance to the hero approaching first an altar and then a seated god [similar in appearance to the sky-giant or man-aspect of the dragon].

Boxing Analysis: The boxing hero wears gauntlets and is built like the classic Near Eastern strong-man/wrestler. The guards are extended, with clenched fists pointed at the head. This, along with the fact that the hero has his head pulled back suggests a low regard for body punching –though punching the "body" of the giant's chariot would not appear to be a practical application of the fistic art! Most notable is the fact that three of the combatants' four fists are pronated, indicating an art that is at least one evolutionary step removed from its fencing or wrestling origins.

Ritual Interpretation: The author is of the opinion that the boxing scene links man's religious observations with the power of the sky-god [who is more similar in appearance to the supplicant and hero than to the seated god and giant]. Whether the hero's opponent is meant to be a sky-giant in a monstrous chariot or a dragon with a human aspect, he is definitely combating a supernatural force on earth linked with acts of worship and the activities of chariot-riding deities. The author regards this association of boxing with chariot-borne gods [deified ancestors?] as an intriguing clue as to the ultimate origin of boxing in the Near East.

Might Makes Right

"Although he is the protector of Uruk's wall and sanctuary,
He oppresses the people; yet he is strong, handsome and wise.
His lust has not spared a mother's chaste daughter
Or spared a warrior's girl-child, or spared a hero's promised bride."

—*The Epic of Gilgamesh*

"It may be that men were intrinsically no more violent than they are today. Yet their acceptance, even celebration, of force as the final arbiter of human affairs is striking."

—Robert L. O'Connell, *Of Arms and Men*

The *Epic of Gilgamesh* provides—taken from his subjects' point-of-view—a literary echo of civil brutality that screams injustice and outrage across the millennia; a brand of injustice that is none-the-less accepted by a fatalistic people. Head-of-state as corrupt cop, fat-cat, celebrity, rapist, kidnapper and thug seems to have been a price most ancients were willing to pay to avoid slaughter by the marauders of the wild lands and enslavement by those nasty neighbors up river. In such a social context something like boxing is bound to emerge as a potent manhood ritual. Boxing—in its many forms—is all about *might* making *right* within accepted limits.

As the centuries of tyranny, war, and oppression grind by under our scrutinizing gaze, we shall witness, through the eyes of the prize-fighter and his spectators and commentators, the reoccurrence of a truly profound phenomena; the embracing of boxing as a life-affirming ritual enjoyed by the righteously mighty and the wronged meek alike.

Chapter 8
Boxers of Egypt –2000 to 1151 B.C.

There is a strong hint of boxing in Pre-*Hellenistic* Egypt. Temples and tombs are decorated with pictures of wrestling and fencing –the activities that gave rise to boxing in its modern form in the streets of 17th Century London. The very symbol that identifies "man in all his actions" in the sacred carvings [*hieroglyphics*] of the Egyptian priesthood is of a half-seated figure with torso turned obliquely and fists raised in a classic bare-knuckle pose.*

There is also the certainty of intimate contact with two known boxing cultures: the Babylonian culture of Mesopotamia from where the first evidence of formalized fist fighting may be found; and the Minoan culture of Crete which is known to have developed a wider variety of fist-fighting rituals than any Western society before or since. However, we only have a handful of actual boxing records from ancient Egypt, which conceal as much as they reveal, and leave us groping in the dark once more for a sure origin of the sport of boxing.

Common Life in Egypt c. 1350 B.C.

Life in Egypt [Greek for Riverland] was undoubtedly better for ordinary people, and kings for that matter, than life in Mesopotamia. The country was ruled by a God-King rather than a Priest-King, who most folks appear to have supported either by working on small family farms and giving a portion to a tax collector, or working as a specialized laborer or craftsman living on or near the worksite. Although life was not as brutal as in Mesopotamia there was still a vast disparity in wealth between the rich and poor, who actually lived in close proximity. Virtually all of the tombs of the god-kings were ransacked by commoners, sometimes the very workmen who had constructed the tombs.

The Egyptian state was constructed atop an ethnically and religiously diverse population [by ancient standards], and its massive bureaucracy waged a war of terror on the general population. Warriors were hired from barbarian tribes to administer an array of grisly punishments: a caning for failing to pay taxes; five maiming face cuts for failure to revere the God-King and/or the gods; and impalement for heresy and other crimes against the state or the state religion. The nation generally prospered when there was a strong God-King so it seems that the common man's resentment was largely focused on the massive and corrupt bureaucracy.

The one thing that everyone in Egypt had in common was there tie to the Nile. The river made their lives possible almost every year, but in some years brought disaster.

Wrestlers, boxers and stick-fighters seem to have been members of the military, which was drawn from a wide base. This indicates that an ordinary soldier, who did well boxing, might come to the attention of the God-King and be able to improve his station in life.

Map 3.
The Rise of War Arts in Ancient Egypt, 2000 to 1151B.C.

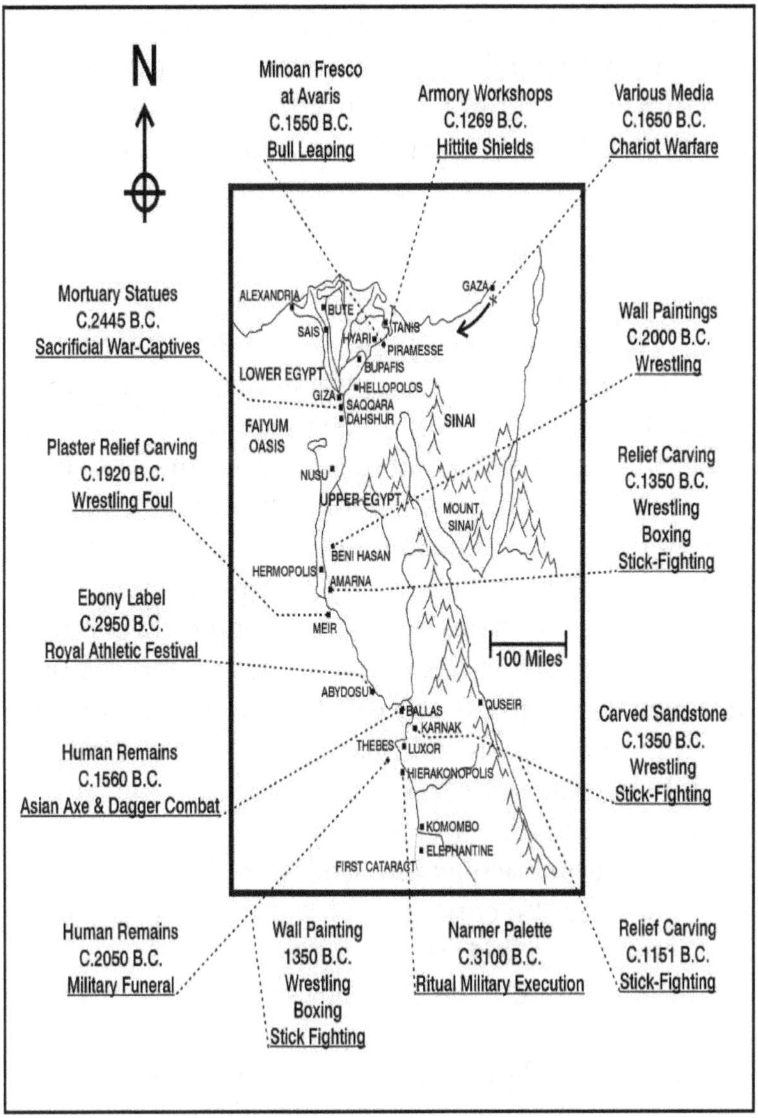
N
Minoan Fresco
at Avaris
C.1550 B.C.
Bull Leaping
Armory Workshops
C.1269 B.C.
Hittite Shields
Various Media
C.1650 B.C.
Chariot Warfare
Mortuary Statues
C.2445 B.C.
Sacrificial War-Captives
Wall Paintings
C.2000 B.C.
Wrestling
Plaster Relief Carving
C.1920 B.C.
Wrestling Foul
Relief Carving
C.1350 B.C.
Wrestling
Boxing
Stick-Fighting
Ebony Label
C.2950 B.C.
Royal Athletic Festival
Carved Sandstone
C.1350 B.C.
Wrestling
Stick-Fighting
Human Remains
C.1560 B.C.
Asian Axe & Dagger Combat
Human Remains
C.2050 B.C.
Military Funeral
Wall Painting
1350 B.C.
Wrestling
Boxing
Stick Fighting
Narmer Palette
C.3100 B.C.
Ritual Military Execution
Relief Carving
C.1151 B.C.
Stick-Fighting
ALEXANDRIA
BUTE
SAIS
HYARI
TANIS
PIRAMESSE
GAZA
LOWER EGYPT
BUPAFIS
HELLOPOLOS
GIZA
SAQQARA
DAHSHUR
SINAI
FAIYUM
OASIS
NUSU
UPPER EGYPT
MOUNT
SINAI
BENI HASAN
HERMOPOLIS
AMARNA
MEIR
100 Miles
ABYDOSU
BALLAS
QUSEIR
KARNAK
THEBES
LUXOR
HIERAKONOPOLIS
KOMOMBO
ELEPHANTINE
FIRST CATARACT

The evidence of boxing and other forms of martial activity in ancient Egypt suggests the possibility of an extremely ancient form of indigenous bare-knuckle folk-boxing or temple-boxing that may have risen, thrived, and died without ever having a significant effect on the mainstream of Near-Eastern and Greco-Roman boxing traditions.

The Question of Egyptian Boxing

Although some boxing historians contend that boxing originated in Egypt and spread to other regions there is no convincing evidence that boxing in Egypt predated boxing in Mesopotamia or Crete.

Other boxing historians contend that boxing originated in Mesopotamia—which is far from certain—and that the practice of boxing then spread to Egypt, from where it spread to Crete and thence to Greece and Rome. There is no indication among sources presently extant that any Egyptian martial arts—much less boxing—spread to Crete. In fact formalized Cretan boxing appears to predate Egyptian boxing by some 300 years.

That fact brings into question the scheme of this book; for the contentious author has placed Egyptian boxing before Cretan boxing in the chronology of boxing history. The reason for the placement of Egypt ahead of Crete in the evolutionary scheme of boxing development is that there are indications in the archaeological record that the Egyptian warrior class practice the boxing related arts of wrestling and stick-fighting before the palatial period of Cretan history when boxing thrived, and that the Egyptian priesthood had at an early date—before the period of Cretan boxing—internalized metaphoric concepts that have since correlated with wide spread folk-boxing in other cultures.

Egypt had all of the ingredients necessary to nurture a strong boxing tradition, and does not appear to have exported her martial arts. Although the possibility of Egyptian boxing being of the greatest antiquity remains, there is no indication that the Minoan-Greco-Roman boxing traditions were descended from an Egyptian model. However, as will be discussed in *All-Power-Fighting: A Fighter's View of MMA from Achilles to Alexander*, pre-Hellenistic Egypt did have some effect on the conduct and development of Classical Greek combat sports. The evidence is present in Herodotus' *Inquires*.

Although Pharaonic Egypt may have harbored the earliest boxing tradition, and perhaps the longest lived bare-knuckle boxing tradition in all of Western and Eastern history, the author is simply unable to prove these suppositions with the meager evidence at hand. In summation, Egypt appears to be an ancient, intriguing, mysterious, dead-end footnote to the story of boxing.

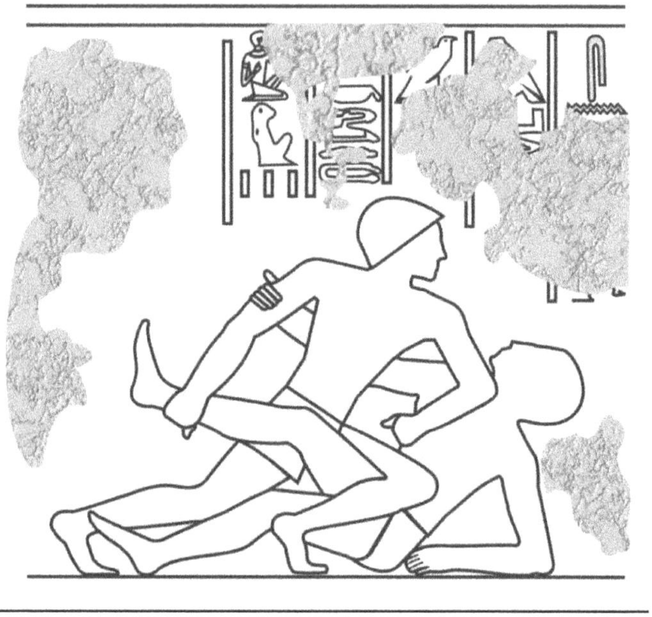

Figure 10.
The Wrestling Foul
From a plaster relief carving, Tomb Chapel of Senbi, Meir, Egypt, c.1920 B.C.

The helmeted head of the top man suggests the possibility of a stick-fighting bout gone to the ground or even some type of military mixed martial art. Therefore, this scene cannot be confidently classified as a depiction of a wrestling match.

This illustration suggests the possible origin of boxing in more than one culture. One might say that wrestling fouls have supplied the boxer with most of his tool kit both foul and fair. If such a tactic was widespread or notable enough to be enshrined in art intended for the high and mighty of Egypt, than this implies a boxing tradition that coexisted or grew out of a more popular and respectable wrestling tradition. The military rulers of ancient societies favored the use of wrestling as a conditioning tool for their troops over boxing because it was less injurious—especially of the hands which are needed for weapon work—and is also more applicable to a military fencing situation were clinching may be frequent and empty-hand striking would generally be futile.

The elbow is delivered with a clenched fist, indicating that the elbow shot may have been a follow-up blow to a hook punch [such as the elbows landed by Julio Caesar Chavez against Meldrick Taylor, circa 1990].

When I view this piece I just know in my bones that the Egyptians must have been boxing or practicing MMA at this time. I just can't prove it.

Figure 11.
The Egyptian Jab
From a relief carving, tomb of Merire II, El Amarna, Egypt, c.1350 B.C.

I love these guys!

This is about as nasty as it gets.

These may be disarmed stick-fighters slugging it out [indicated by the helmet on the left most fighter]. As it stands the right-most man is advancing with a long posted lunge with hands up and is eating a right rear-hand jab [similar to that used by Lightweight Champion Kosta Tzyu against Ben Tacky in 2002] from the left-most man, who is posting his straight punch with a shorter step and is covering with an open lead left hand. This may represent a foiled clinch attempt.

The right hand of each fighter appears to be formed into a spear-hand [familiar to modern gung fu and karate practitioners]. However, due to the nature of the surviving art, and the fact that it has been interpreted by two successive illustrators, this may simply represent an unintentional distortion of the record. The author does side with the spear-hand interpretation of the blow because it is obviously being used in a fencing context, and more pure forms of Egyptian boxing do feature attention to vital point striking.

Fighting For the Intercessor: A Warrior's Sacred Duty 1353 B.C.

"You sit...a chariot-warrior who fights to uphold my rule...the possessor of a woman from Babylon, and a servant from Byblos, of a young maiden from Alalakh, and of an old lady from Arapkha."

-a letter from Amenhotep II to Usersatet at Semna

He admired the stunningly painted brick pavilion where he would soon fight to sanctify the victory celebration of his war-lord, the Third Amenhotep, God-King of Riverland. This would be the most important fight of his life; and it would not be waged with bow and sword aboard his swift chariot against the enemy, but with his naked fists against a war-brother. Their Lord had finally grown old—even now his son was assuming the reigns of kingship—and would soon ascend to The Distant One, to intercede for all who tend and protect Riverland. The fights with fist and stick conducted after the dance of supplicants would be the last combats over which their warlord would preside in this life. For this reason he and the other fighters had been carefully chosen from amongst the battle-veterans and matched to insure that each and every combat would be fought with reverence...

His opponent was a strong Up-river Man, and it was an honor to be assigned such a fighter. The Delta Men were the most skilled fist-fighters, but the Up-river Men were favored by the gods for their war-spirit.

He would normally circle right in camp bouts against such a fearsome opponent—not today. This fight was before the gods and he posted a hard left snake jab to the chest. Before his short hard lunge could sink in he took a forearm smash between the eyes. Sparks arced from his eyes as he was rocked back heavily on his heels and cool blood flooded his throbbing sockets. Half blind from the blood, he heard more than felt a fist crunch into his chin. A priest's voice cried out "Strike! Hit him."

His sight was blurred, but he knew his man was using a very high guard. So he answered with a strong right to his opponent's floating rib, which brought a pleasing gasp. However, before he could retract his fist the Up-river Man's forearm block came down late, catching him at the wrist joint and breaking the thumb at its base. The punches came slower now, though he had little left to retaliate with—his right hand heavy and useless. As the taller man came in for another series of pawing jabs and hammer fists he stepped on line and posted a long hard jab, with his fingers in the shape of the spear. The big man lurched forward and bent over his lead knee as he clutched at his dangling eye-lid. He grimaced in pain and his eye-ball showed large and white in its socket.

The High Priest stepped forward and sanctified the combat, and the acolytes attended to the Up-river Man. As he stood upon the blood-soaked bricks on unsteady legs, the Intercessor signaled approval. At that moment he addressed The Distant One in silence, for the sake of his children. It would be the most he could ever give. The Distant One was watching. It comforted him to know, that after this honorable victory, his heart would be that much lighter, when finally, after his death, it was placed on the Scale of Oblivion.

Figure 12-A
Amenhotep III, God-King of Egypt, First Known Boxing Promoter, depicted celebrating his third royal jubilee in 1353 B.C, at which he presided over no less than four bare-knuckle bouts.

Wall painting from the tomb of the royal steward Kheruef (TT 192), at Thebes, Egypt, circa 1350 B.C.

Figure 12-B
The Champions of Amenhotep III

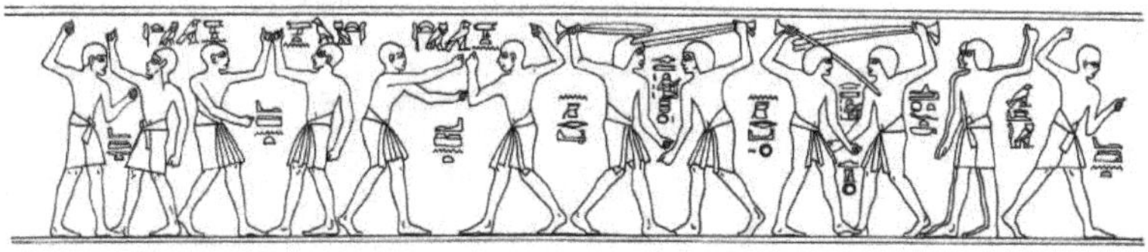

Boxers and fencers competing at the third royal jubilee [sed-festival] of Amenhotep III, in 1353 B.C., at the painted mud-brick jubilee pavilion at Kom el-Samak [now destroyed]. From a panel of a wall painting from the tomb of Kheruef (TT 192) at Thebes, Egypt c. 1350 B.C.

The author's tactical deductions of the six pairs of fighters proceed from left to right. These conclusions were purposely deduced independent of the translation of the accompanying hieroglyphics, and are the result of a strictly bio-mechanic reading of the figures. Since the rightmost fighter in each of the 6 panels is depicted as a southpaw, it is assumed that this represents an artistic convention for showing the chest of each fighter.

Pair 1: The rightward fighter has attempted to step forward with a lead hammer-fist. His attempt is frustrated by the opponent who takes a short slide-step, catching the supporting wrist of the hammer-blow with his skull, while sneaking a jab into the exposed armpit, followed up by a rear-hand hammer-fist to the face.

Pair 2: The leftmost fighter advances with a lead hammer-fist, which is blocked by the opponent with a hammer-fist block. He appears ready to shift his right leg foreword under a rising jab to the armpit or face or an uppercut to the body.

Pair 3: Both fighters advance; the leftmost cautiously behind a one-two combination, and his opponent aggressively behind a high hammer-guard in anticipation of smashing a rear-hand hammer-fist into his opponent's face, neck or collarbone.

Pair 4: Both stick-fighters advance; the leftmost fencer with a forehand, while his opponent covers with a roof-block—though his attempt at taking the inside clinch position on the low-line seems frustrated by left's superior empty-hand positioning.

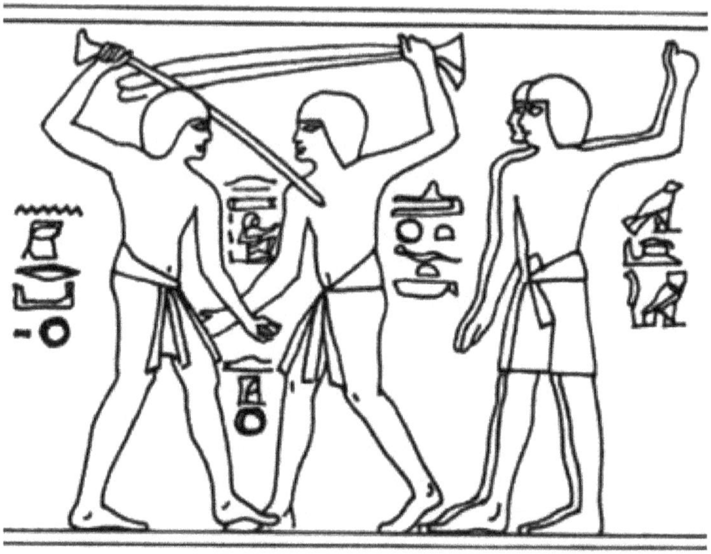

Pair 5: The rightmost fencer advances with a hard forehand possibly in anticipation of a clinch or hip-throw. However, his attack is frustrated by left stepping on his lead foot and covering with a roof-block as he positions for a groin or gut punch with his empty hand.

Note: The two figures standing by may be coaches, but appear to be seconds as they are helmeted like the fencers. Their different sashes may indicate a lesser or greater rank. Perhaps they are fighters coaching their teammates?

Pair 6: This pair is incomplete, however it appears to be a more highly charged version of the encounter in Pair 1, with the unseen opponent's posture assumed to be a leading hammer fist that would expose the armpit.
The leftmost fighter is stepping hard with a jab—possibly with a pointed thumb—to the armpit of his opponent, no doubt ready to follow up with a hammer-fist.

Stylistic points: The boxing style is obviously derived or influenced by the fencing. The chief blows are the hammer-fist and the vertical jab, which—if the pointed thumb is representative of the combats and not an artistic convention—may indicate attention to vital-point striking. The chief defense is the high forearm guard and stepping in on the half-beat to jam a high strike, which is evocative of stick-fencing. The stick-fencing itself is highly evolved with attention to clinching and empty-hand striking evident.

Overall Notes: Pairs 1 and 6 and the fencing seconds are wearing less ornate sashes, which may indicate junior status. The physiques are realistic and the faces individualized, indicating a record of actual individual participants. The left most fighter of each pair appears to be the more skilled or most savvy of the two.

Figure 13.
The Spirit of the Fist in Riverland

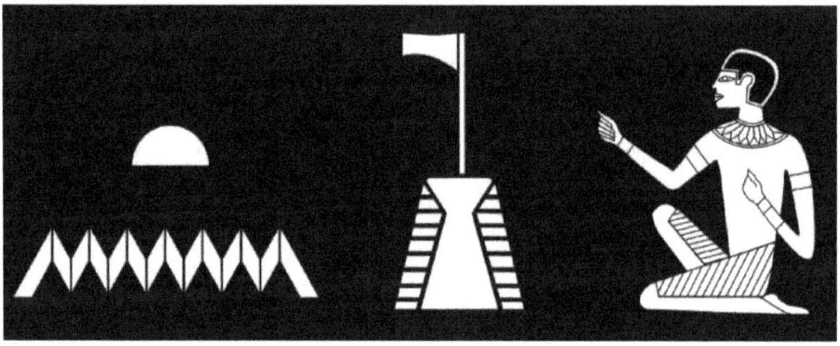

With a deep history of mass-gatherings to erect monuments that remain breathtakingly huge even by modern standards, and to celebrate the most anxiously awaited harvests of antiquity, along with an ancient tradition of sacred picture writing that depicted man at his most basic in a pugilistic pose, it may well be that the land of the great pyramids hosted the best-attended boxing matches in human history.

We just can't know for sure, so we will have to settle for wondering about that long-dead past, and hoping for newly discovered records of the bare-knuckle boxers of ancient Egypt.

Chapter 9
Sacred War Art: The Boxing Warriors of Crete—1700 to 1380 B.C.

> Meriones, great dancer that you are
> Had I shafted you my spear would have finally
> Ended your dancing."
> -Homer, *The Iliad*

The passage above, written some 800 years after the heyday of Cretan boxing, reflects the importance of war dancing in that culture, as Aeneas, the second hero of Troy [and mythical ancestor of the Romans], chants his frustration at his lithe Cretan rival Meriones, who appears to be a renowned arrow-dancer. In fact, numerous passages in *The Iliad* describe the spear dodging ability of Meriones and his Cretan lord Idomeneus.

The *kouretes* was a Cretan military dance based on an ancient arrow-dodging drill. Throughout the Archaic, Classical and Hellenistic periods of Greek life the Cretans were renowned archers, dancers, cheaters, liars, soldiers-for-hire, and crafty boxers, one of whom was fined for killing an opponent at Olympia. To call someone a Cretin is, to this day, an insult that denies his honor and integrity—and there was just something creepy about the Cretans that the mainland Greeks never seemed able to shake. Perhaps it was a distant memory of a mysterious island kingdom, ruled by pirate chieftains, who paid homage to their unforgiving gods and goddesses with the sacrifice of youthful victims in brutal temple combats, and bizarre bull-leaping rituals.

Whether or not the reality of Cretan boxing and bull-leaping was as sinister as hinted at above is uncertain. However, the boxers of Crete have been immortalized in fabulously carved and painted stone, and the aspects of their fistic rituals appear to the modern mind to be as ritualistically brutal as any Roman arena combat of late antiquity; and, most stunning of all, appear to have been conducted indoors, in sacred temple precincts.

So, if the reader would like to savor the flavor of Cretan boxing in a modern context: imagine the toughest welterweights and middleweights from New York and D.C. meeting in Philadelphia to fight to the finish by candlelight with MMA gloves; before the altar of an old catholic church; the corner-men are altar boys doped-up on prescription painkillers; the ref is a priest; the judges are nuns who are drunk on opium-infused wine; and the ring-card girls are topless female rodeo pros...

I don't know about you, but I'm there!

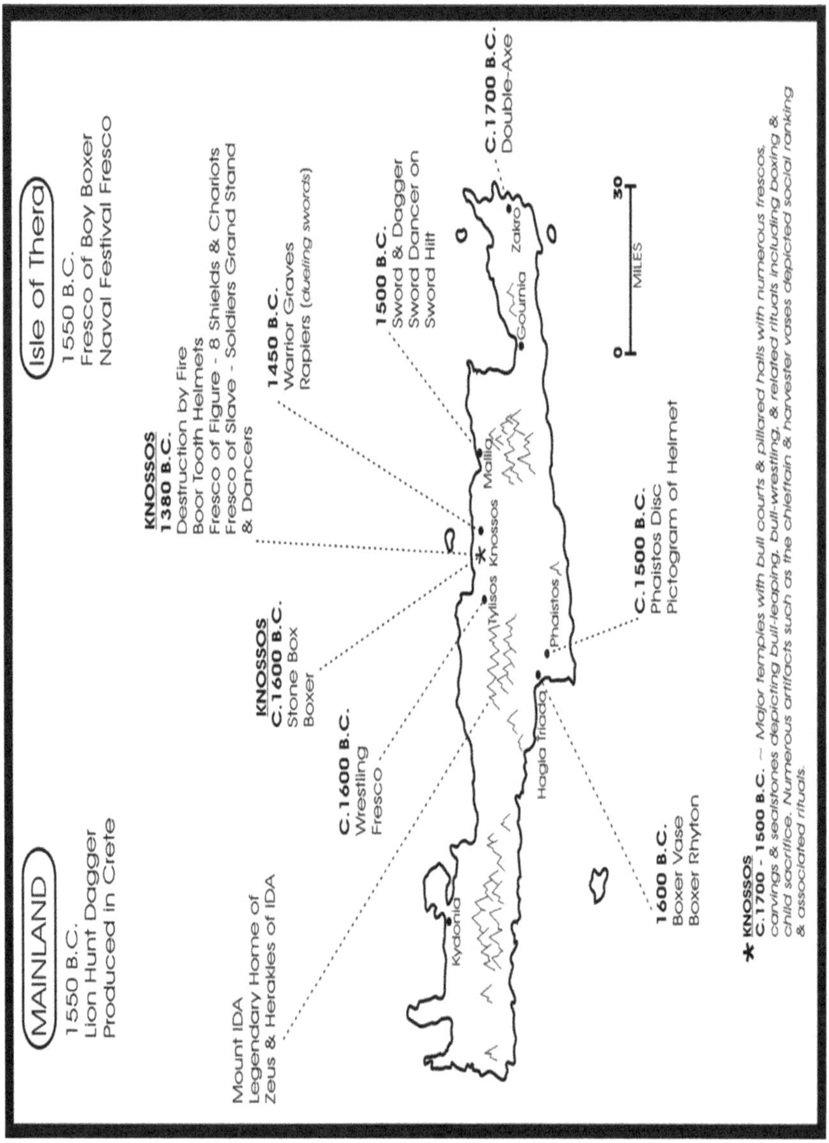

Map 4.
The Rise of War Arts in Ancient Crete –1700 to 1380 B.C.

The war arts of Crete seem to be equal part indigenous and import. The author believes that the indigenous aspects of the Cretan martial arts [bull-leaping, and a uniquely brutal form of boxing] constituted sacred rites rather than popular past-times.

The Mystery of Cretan Boxing

"What emerges from the archaeology is a culture steeped in religion."
-Rodney Castleden, *Minoans*

Boxing on the isle of Crete appears to emerge whole, in a wide variety of brutal forms, circa 1700 B.C. with the rise of the second phase of the Palatial Era which began circa 1900 B.C. and would be extinguished by 1380. Boxing spanned from 1700 through 1500, or the 200 year peak that saw the archeological period known as middle Minoan IIIA through Late Minoan IB. In other words boxing rose and declined as part of a unique burst of religious and cultural activity between two great disasters; a period of invasion, social upheaval or natural disaster around 1900 B.C., and the eruption of the nearby volcanic Isle of Thera around 1500 B.C.

The fistic activity depicted is being practiced in a religious context by members of a warrior class, as well as children. These forms of boxing may have served several purposes: initiation of the warrior class; religious celebrations, and human sacrifice: lethal [resulting in death]; or symbolic [resulting in a knockout]. The author assumes that boxing served all of these ritualistic needs; either as a progression with the initiate advancing to progressively more lethal bouts, or as three or four related forms of boxing that served different functions; initiating the young, conditioning of military men, providing an alternative to dueling among the officer class, and possibly as a purely religious expression or sacrifice.

Although some have made the case for the importation of Egyptian martial arts along with trade goods, this author thinks it most likely that boxing –if it did not originate in Crete—was imported from Anatolia [modern Turkey] or even mainland Greece. It is the author's opinion that Cretan boxing represented one of three independent ancient Western boxing traditions that developed at roughly the same time [2000-1700 B.C.] under similar ecological and military pressures: Anatolian and Mesopotamian boxing based on belt wrestling; Egyptian boxing based on stick-fighting and submission wrestling; and Cretan or Minoan boxing based on military fencing [probably with bronze cut & thrust swords] in association with bull-fighting.

All of the above forms of boxing became prominent after the rise of chariot warfare, and *may* have had a primal root tradition among the Indo-European peoples that appear to have first developed chariot warfare. In any case, all of these fighting forms are unique enough to have formed independently of the others. With Cretan boxing, though, we are possibly being treated to our first view of a continuous ancient boxing tradition, because the boxing of Crete and Greece are probably descended from a common Balkan or Anatolian root tradition.

As for the boxers of Crete, we cannot know who they were, and can only conjecture as to why they fought, but we have a good idea as to where their bouts were staged, and brilliant carvings indicating precisely how they went about their brutal business.

We are about to get a peek at one of the most remarkable martial arts traditions in human history. This is a snapshot of boxing among a matriarchal society that had yet to abandon the goddess, and who enjoyed naval superiority across the Middle Sea.

Figure 14.
A Boxer of Knossos
Carving on fragment of steatite [stone] pyxis [box], from Knossos c.1600 B.C.

This is a boxer of the first grade: a man who fights naked except for his codpiece [groin-protector] and diadem [metal head-band]. His boxing gauntlet appears to consist of leather wraps from hand to elbow with a bronze knuckle plate. He appears to be posing in the victory stance over a fallen opponent whose knee is pictured in the foreground.

As indicated by the victory pose, Cretan boxers were flat-footed power punchers who posted a hard “corkscrew” [hyper-pronated] jab to the chin or chest and followed up with hard uppercuts and straight rights to the body and face. The chambered position of the rear hand on the hip is standard and is very similar to traditional Okinawin and Japanese karate. This primitive power-punching technique [a karate reverse-punch] may indicate a young art [perhaps as young as 3 generations], and, along with the almost total lack of evasive footwork, and a low guard, would certainly account for the insanely high 100% knockout ratio depicted in the surviving art from Crete proper [Later art under Minoan influence from Thera and Cyprus does not indicate the same robotic lack of finesse.]

The Leather-bound Fist: "Taping" the Hands for Ancient Boxing

To a modern boxer hand wrapping is simple injury prevention. For those ancient boxers who wrapped their hands, injury prevention was certainly a concern. For Minoan boxers, who were the first known fighters to protect their hands, injury prevention was simply one of many functions served by their hand gear. Soft leather hand straps were used throughout the history of ancient boxing to protect the hands; overlaid by injury inflicting gauntlets in competition, or soft gloves for sparring, or used alone.

From June 1999 to June 2005 this author used 3 different types of leather hand straps. The best thing about leather wraps is that they never develop a stink like fabric wraps and do not require washing. Applying oil when the wrap begins to dry and hanging them between uses are the only maintenance required. The worst thing about leather wraps is that they come undone easily, even when tightly tied. Basically, any strap that is over a half inch wide is going to buckle and unravel often, especially around the knuckles. It is particularly difficult to wrap the thumb with leather in such a way that it will not unravel after a few defensive uses of the open hand. On the plus side, even thin narrow leather straps offer more protection against impact than fabric.

The most efficient use of leather hand straps is to use 10 to 12 feet of half-inch wide by 1/16th inch thick soft leather for the knuckles and back of the hand, starting at the palm and terminating around the wrist. The base of the thumb and the nerve center behind it, and the bones of the wrist up to mid forearm may then be protected by a 6 foot length of 2 inch wide by 1/8th inch thick leather, looped and crossed around the thumb [like a modern wrap], and then spiraled down the wrist in 1 inch increments and tied down with raw hide. Such a heavy wrist wrap encourages the kind of passive covering guard often seen in modern amateur and late Archaic Greek boxing [c. 550 B.C.].

A tight-fisted karate-like use of the forearm as a shield also seems to have been the trend in Minoan boxing, obviously encouraged by the additional forearm plate.

The offensive use of the hand strap as a weapon is limited to using the edges of the wrap to slice open the opponent, and allowing these edges to grow abrasive by not cleaning or oiling them, and allowing the accumulated body salts of many training sessions, and the crusting action of dried blood to further roughen those segments of the wrap that cover the striking areas of the fist.

As boxing was introduced into Anatolia, Mesopotamia and possibly Crete by Indo-European invaders, it is possible that hand wrapping with the skin of a sacrificial ox may have its origin as a cult ritual [wraps of fleece or linen could have been used to protect the hand] rather than as a practical measure. Among the Indo-Europeans the true word for hand was taboo and unspoken and each people used their own euphemistic term for hand. This appears to have been associated with a primal cult dedicated to a "god with the large hand", often pictured with a long arm. The use of sacrificial bull hides in Druidic divinations and the strong association of Zeus, Apollo, Herakles and Theseus [all deities variously credited with the original Greek boxing contests and having deep cultic links to the bull] lends strength to the cultic significance of leather hand strapping.

*Ellis, Peter Berresford. The Druids, Constable and Company, London, 1994, pages 126 and 222

Figure 15.
The Boxer Vase
black steatite [stone] vase, Hagia Triada, Crete,
c.1600 B.C.

The Boxer Vase

The boxer vase is the single richest ancient boxing find recovered to date. The composition of the vase definitely presents boxing as a religious activity, as it is closely associated -perhaps even integrated—with the Minoan bull-leaping ritual, which appears to have been the most celebrated religious rite of ancient Crete.

One may read the vase as a record of a single event with concurrent rituals being conducted according to their social or religious status. [The bull-leaping appears to have been witnessed by crowds of up to 600 spectators.*] Alternately, one might read the vase as a guide to an individual's upward progress through the social-religious hierarchy by completing a series of violent rituals, most of which consist of boxing bouts. In either case what we have here are three grades of boxer:

3rd are the unprotected youths, possibly the sons of the wealthy** or "amateurs" or possibly untried -though trained—initiates

2nd are the helmeted boxers, possibly military men** or "professionals"

1st are the plumed boxers, possibly chiefs, princes, or "champions"

Both sets of helmeted boxers combat amongst pillars, definitely placing them inside.

It is the author's opinion that the plumed boxers are men of both military and noble status that qualify to fight as the diademed boxer depicted in Figure 14. This theory supposes the following ritual progression: long-haired youths of noble birth fight bare-knuckle for the right to hold a military command; military commanders fight helmeted with gauntlets in elimination bouts for the right to fight as plumed boxers; the two finalists among the helmeted class fight with gauntlets in plumed helmets for the right to fight the king or champion; finally, the victor will fight the king or champion to the death with gauntlets wearing only the ceremonial diadem. According to this scheme the plumed and diademed boxers would both be regarded as being of the 1st grade.

The youthful boxers and the bull-leaper perform in an open space, either outside, or [more likely] on the broad palace*** dance floor reserved for bull-sports and dancing.

*Castleden, *Minoans*, page 28. Crowd estimates by Evans based on analysis of a grandstand fresco.
**Castledon, *Minoans*, page 166, The Chieftain Cup. Depiction of noblemen as longhaired with ankle wraps, and military men as short-haired with no ankle wraps covering their boot uppers correspond with youthful boxers with wrapped ankles and helmeted boxers with unwrapped ankles on the Boxer Vase. Interestingly the plumed [the plumes possibly being symbolic of long hair] boxers have the same footwear as the youths.
*** Castelden, *Minoans*, pages 123-57, Castleden makes a definitive case for the Minoan "palaces" having actually been temples dominated by economically potent priestesses.

Figure 16.
The Youthful Boxers

The youthful bare-knuckle boxers depicted at the base of the vase appear to be fighting on the dance-floor of the sacred bull court either as part of an event preliminary to the bull-rites and/or as a rite of passage that would qualify them for participation in the bull-rites and/or more lethal forms of boxing. Perhaps these youths are sacrificial victims taken as hostages from tributary nations such as the mythic Athens of Theseus?

Though these boxers wear no hand or head protection, they do have groin-protectors and sport long hair –both indications of free or noble status among the Minoans. Although this does not rule them out as hostages or sacrifices it does indicate that they were probably initiates, who had not yet earned a helmet or diadem.

This panel may depict two combats with two victors pictured in triumph to left and right. But it appears more likely that the panel is meant to be read from left to right as a record of a single combat, during which the loser either attempts to kick from the floor as he is being punched or tumbles backward as the result of a blow or blows.

Significantly the lead fist of the victor is pointed down at the kicking boxer's face* in the first action panel and he appears to stand victorious before and after the two-scene bout, indicating that he has been victorious in a previous bout and/or that his opponent was foredoomed to defeat.

*Indicating the "legal" punching of downed fighters as in later Greek submission boxing and early American gloved boxing [Jack Dempsey hovered over his fallen victims and beat them as they attempted to rise, and Jack Johnson punched from the floor to good effect against Stanley Ketchel in their filmed championship bout in 1909].

Figure 17.
The Armored Boxers

These boxers of the second grade appear to be battling in a pillared cult room or crypt possibly adjoining the bull-court. The technique is the same as that demonstrated by the boxer of Knossos and the youthful boxers in the panel below [illustration 16]. The progress of the combat also seems to be similar to the youthful combat with the second half only of this bout being depicted. The loser is first shone reclining before a pillar in the partial frame to the left and is then depicted attempting to rise with the aid of his clenched fists [a posture familiar to modern boxing fans] as his opponent hovers over him with downward-turned lead fist aimed at his exposed lower back, possibly for a kidney blow.

Significantly these boxers are helmeted in headgear better suited for military fencing –

indicated by the cheek pieces—than a boxing style dominated by linear punching techniques; and are striking with hand gear that offers more wrist protection than knuckle coverage –again indicating gear intended for military fencing.*

*Military fencing forms usually feature attention to the thrust, secondary to the dominant slash. The types of bronze cut-and-thrust swords excavated at Minoan sites would have been used in a similar fashion by ancient duelists. Four millennia later the lethality of such a dueling weapon in the hands of an argumentative officer class lead at least one British monarch to promote boxing as an alternative to the sword duel in order to preserve a viable leadership pool.

Figure 18.
The Plumed Boxers

These heavy-muscled boxers* of the first grade are actually engaged in a competitive bout in the first damaged frame. They are both turned southpaw having advanced with lunging steps in a "linear karate walk". The leftmost boxer appears to be posting a stiff right jab to the face of his opponent as he eats a left uppercut to the belt line.

The second frame appears to depict the leftward boxer's further advance –in two stages—in a karate stepping motion. He apparently hurt his opponent with the loaded right lead to the face, followed up with left step and left uppercut, and is finishing the other boxer [who is taking a knee after turning away] with a right hook delivered with a right step.

The second frame might alternatively by interpreted as the injured fighter being punched from behind as he turns away while flailing with a hook –with the loser or victor taking a knee comprising a third frame—although the footwork for this interpretation is not convincingly depicted by the artist.

Overall this panel retains the two basic themes of the diademed and armored bouts: the victor enters from stage left; and he wins by knockout by shifting all of his body weight into each blow by stepping with the supporting leg and pushing off with the foot [*posting*, albeit it flat-footed] of the other leg.

The attention to athletic details portraying simultaneous strikes –rare in any ancient or modern fight illustration—and the strain on the thighs of the hard punching fighters has convinced the author that the Boxer Vase depicts actual events, and that the two fighters pictured in the top panel were both regarded as important individuals by the artist as well as those who commissioned the work.

*The fighters are built like modern middleweight or light-heavyweight boxers.

Figure 19.
The Crypt of the Waning King
Artist's conception, Knossos, c.1600 B.C.

A bout between two diademed boxers of the 1st grade being witnessed by a priestesses of the Snake Goddess, a priestess of the Poppy Goddess, and a priest of the Master of Animals. The fighter to the left represents the reigning king attempting to qualify for another eight-year reign against a younger opponent that has been chosen by the high priestesses to be his imminent successor.

The "waning king" is using his lead arm for angular blocks, which would cause the blows to be deflected by his bronze arm-plate. This interpretation of the Cretan bent-arm lead was first suggested by Gardiner c.1930, was used by early 20th Century gloved fighters, is a mainstay of Wing Chun gung fu, and is most often used in the modern boxing ring by Thai fighters. This is probably the safest bare-knuckle defense, and, if Gardiner's contention is correct, suggests a bare-knuckle origin for Cretan temple boxing as demonstrated in the bottom panel of the Boxer Vase. If such was the case than the headgear and handgear was probably adapted from contemporary fencing equipment. The ceremonial rhyton [serving cup] held by the priestess of the Poppy Goddess depicts the same ritual progression of boxing and bull-leaping as that depicted on the Boxer Vase.

Map 5.
Palace of the Boxers

Possible crypts and cult rooms where armored bouts may have taken place are indicated as being behind the tripartite shrine. This is conjecture on the part of the author, as the site of these bouts cannot be known for sure at the time of this writing. This is a partial composite layout, based on floor plans of the great temple complexes of Knossos, Zakro, Gournia, Mallia and Phaistos.*

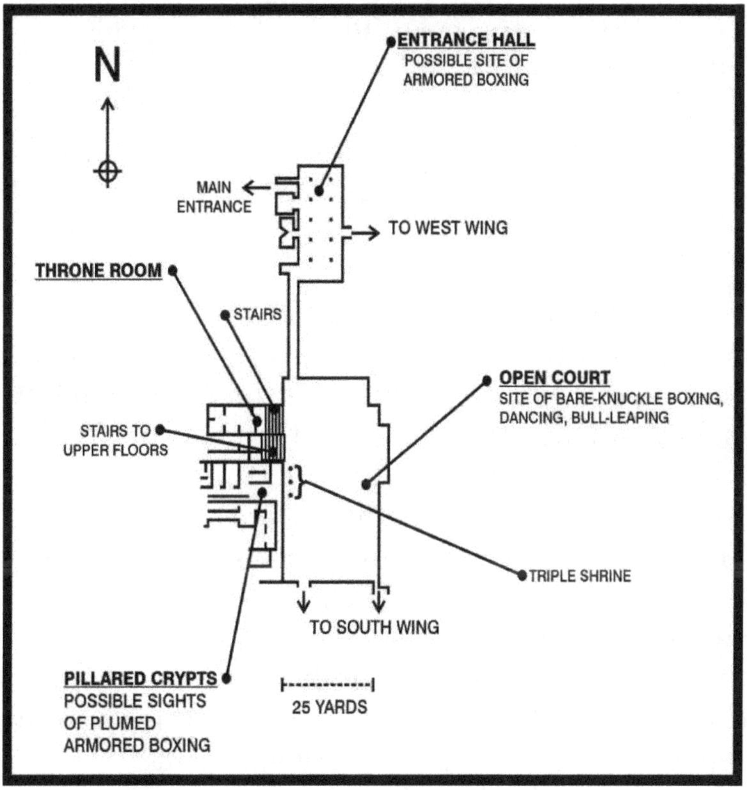

*Willetts, R. F. *The Civilization of Ancient Crete*, Barnes & Noble, NY, [no date available] pages 60, 62, 65, 66, 70

The Waning King: A Fighter's View of His Final Title Fight c. 1600 B.C.

"Do not recoil; tempt mystify and enchant him."
-The Epic of Gilgamesh

He had been a dancer as a boy, a boxer as a youth, a soldier and chieftain as a young man; and now, on this late winter morning, on Ascension Day, eight years into his reign, he would raise his fists for the last time. He stood naked, quietly contemplating his fate in the Advent Chamber. Though the Sun would be showing strongly at this time his world was suffused in darkness; the walls swarming with golden butterflies taking flight from the bronze scales of Fate faintly illuminated by the candles of the Poppy Goddess, who, to this final day, relieved the pain of his battle wounds. In retrospect his life had always been the same, dancing, hurting, being hurt, and seizing victory...until this day.

For most of his reign he imagined that he would seize victory one last time and be the first king to reign twice. But his ministrations with the numerous priestesses had recently been more frequent and more taxing, with some of the Goddesses' Daughters apparently bent on dying in his care. His training had lagged with the increase in demand for his sacraments. He spent his days with the priestesses and his nights drinking to the gods with the priests; his duty as king, his doom as a fighter.

His final sign from Fate was his greeting of the returning ship chiefs at the docks, among them his opponent, a lean young war-fighter offered by the ship chiefs, sanctified by the priests, and accepted by the priestesses for his ability to defeat the old king and bring new life to the temple nursery, as well as new inspiration to the young sea chiefs. He now understood that his true sacrifice as a son of the House of the Double-axe had not been on the ships or on the day of his kingship victory, but today at Ascension.

At birth his parents had named him secretly and his friends had called him Thistle. But since his first victory he had not had a name, only a rank, and the master of ranks—the wise old priest of the ox-glove—had just put an end to his dreaming with his matter-of-fact entrance, "Well, my king, it's time to harness you for that hawk that's just come up from the sea. I know what you're thinking, but you actually have a chance. Not saying it's a big one. These ox-gloves are better than *his*—I know, I just laced him up. Besides, as much as our dear little priestesses have drained you, they'll be a damned distraction for him. He's been at sea six months. All the same, he's got the edge and cruel Mother Fate curses us all. So try your best to look good when the fight gets ugly. The important thing is to be *worthy* when you get to where you're headed."

As the priest worked in silence the thirty-year-old king was once again laced into bronze-plated bull-hide gauntlets, cinched up with a bull-hide cup, crowned with the golden head-band of sacral combat, and given one last piece of advice as he tapped the sacral kingship band on his brow, "Remember, boy, the only time I call a break is when this thing comes off. So when it happens to him, or *you*, breath deep."

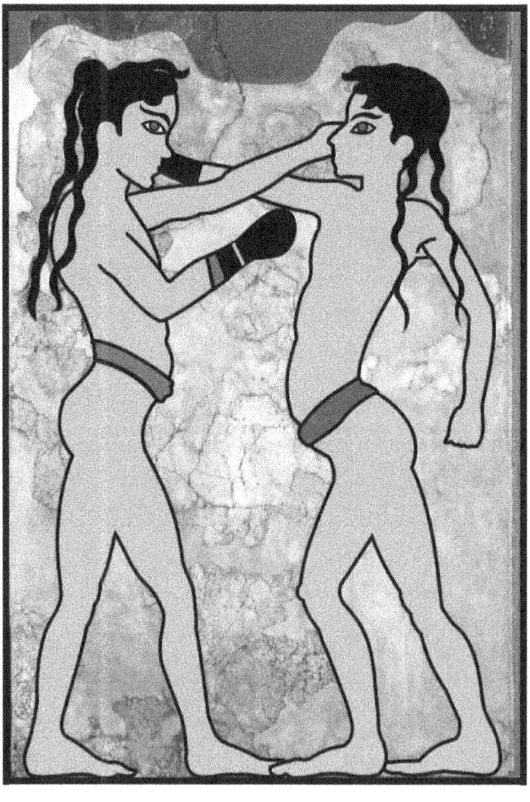

Figure 20.
The Boy Boxers
Illustration based on a wall painting from the isle of Thera, c.1500 B.C.

This appears to be an initiation rite with the leftward boxer showing good form out of a southpaw stance and having his hair braided for the occasion. The other child is eating a straight left as he misses with a wide right out of an orthodox stance. In the author's view the child on the right is being sacrificed to propitiate the gods -who had been angry at about this time, dispensing earthquakes liberally in preparation for the catastrophic eruption of Thera—or has simply been supplied as an easy opponent for the trained boxer's manhood initiation. A third interpretation could be the initiation of the unschooled boy into the art of boxing.

An important element of this scene is the use of what appear to be soft leather boxing gloves as opposed to bronze-plated fencing gauntlets. It seems likely that this scene depicts an unschooled boy boxing with a boy who may represent a 4th grade of boxer. Two other interpretations of this painting have been put forward: one postulating that the right-most boxer is a girl; the other that he is a "kicker" ready to deliver a knee in some sort of primal mixed-martial-arts match. This author disagrees with both of these interpretations as both are punching at close range and both wear girdles.

This image of Minoan child boxers might bring to mind modern junior-Olympians, and remind the student of Greco-Roman history of the many statues proud Greek fathers raised to commemorate their sons' victories at Olympia. However, one should take pause and consider that this beautifully disturbing fresco was painted in a building where evidence of child sacrifice was found, and that the deeply religious people responsible for this art and those sacrifices were receiving dire warning concerning a natural disaster that would soon extinguish their very world.*

In pure athletic terms the technique of the pony-tailed boxer is superior to that of all of the adult male fighters depicted in artifacts recovered from Knossos and Hagia Triada, indicating – especially as this superior form is being demonstrated by a boy in a colonial town—that boxing methods had evolved significantly in the intervening years [about three generations, if a generation is reckoned at 30 years**].

The most curious aspect of this illustration is the hand-gear. Each boy only wears a glove on his right hand. Note that the right-most boy isn't even using his un-gloved left, and, like many a modern novice, is depending exclusively on right hand power punches. The more skilled boxer to the left is leading with the gloved hand and scoring a precise shot with the bare left hand. If one focuses on the hand-gear and technique this strangely erotic picture seems even more brutal. The hand-gear appears to be of soft wrappings under a leather glove. The child on the left has a bronze band on his right wrist and [not depicted in this illustration] on his upper right arm, which may indicate noble status.

*The eruption of Thera has been cited as the possible cause for mythical events as diverse as the plagues of Egypt, the parting of the Red Sea, and the sinking of Atlantis. However, even if it wasn't quite the world shaker some believe, it was certainly a bad day for the people who actually lived on that particular exploding mountain.

**The author reckons athletic generations in terms of a fighter's prime from age 21 to 35, or 15 years, marking two generations of fighters for every [30 year] social generation.

The Nature and Legacy of the Cretan Beast

"My spear and sword and fine shield, which guards my skin,
are my fortune. For I plough with this, reap with this, I tread
the sweet wine from the vine with this, I am master of the slave-farmers
with this. But those who dare not hold the spear and sword and that
fine shield, to guard their skin, all fall and kiss my knee, calling me
master and great lord."

-*The Song of Hybrias*, Cretan lyric poem c.500 B.C.*

By 500 B.C. Crete had become a feuding backwater of Classical Greece populated by brutal clan bosses, crafty boxers, mercenary snipers, and tough mountain shepherds. Despite regarding their Cretan contemporaries with snobbish disdain the philosophers of Athens harbored a dim ancestral memory of a brutal King named Minos who demanded an annual tribute of seven youths and seven maidens to be sacrificed to the Minotaur –a half-man half-bull monster who wandered a labyrinth devouring the children of Athens…

The legend aside, the Cretan Labyrinths [Houses of the Double-Axe] were occupied by shadowy kings henpecked by an order of axe-totting, opium-using priestesses with a penchant for violent sports. These labyrinths were the center of cult activities involving bull-leaping, bull-wrestling, armored boxing, and mass intoxication. This was all supported by a maritime economy [aggressive trading and piracy] operated by some well-armed chieftains who apparently cut their martial teeth pissing-off bulls and boxing the ears off of hand-picked opponents in the labyrinths.

The bull and double-axe were symbols of a nation ruled [or heavily influenced] by women in a man's world. The fact that the Chieftains that these priestesses ruled appear to have been militarily dominant would be more than enough motivation for the woman-scorning mainlanders to blame it all on a mad zoo-keeper. It would also explain why the mainland Greeks appear to have adopted boxing as one of their manhood rituals, even retaining many of the uniquely Cretan aspects of the art, such as wraps, age classes, and beating a fallen foe.

There are many things left to guesswork concerning the character of Cretan boxing:
Were the losers actually executed? Did boxing occur outside of a religious context?

Were they all hopelessly flat-footed? Whatever the hidden truths of Cretan boxing the author is certain that it either formed the basis for Greek boxing or shared a common root tradition.

As for the nature of the temple mazes in connection with boxing, the author believes that young men and women were taken as offerings from tributary states, brought to the temples in sevens [7 being the number of the doomed hero], trained for their lethal rituals, and then either actually or symbolically sacrificed in ritual fist-fights and bull-sports to propitiate the cruelly potent gods of the Minoan world**.

*Certainly evokes the image of a 21st Century rapper lionizing his 9MM handgun.

**Minoan is a modern term. The Egyptians called them Keftiu, the Hebrews called them Caphtorites, and they probably called their home island Kaftor. What they called themselves is uncertain.

Chapter 11
On Hostile Shores: The Riddle of Samson and Goliath –1225 to 1000 B.C.

"I have something to say!
It's better to burnout than to fade away!"
-Kurgan, *Highlander*

The events portrayed in *The Iliad* pertaining to the siege of Troy [Ilium] appear to have occurred about 1220 B.C. The epic itself was not committed to writing by Homer until about 720 B.C. So, what we actually have in *The Iliad* is a composite of events, practices and personas that spanned 500 years. However, *The Iliad* was taken as literal history by the ancients –we should give their opinion some credence—and the archaeological evidence does support the basic story: that a confederation of proto-Greek warlords and their clans waged a wasteful siege against the maritime city of Troy, resulting in Troy's destruction, their loss of power at home due to the protracted nature of the struggle and the stress placed on their feudal economy, and that many –like Odysseus—were left homeless due to barbarian invasions and/or peasant uprisings and adventured around the Mediterranean Sea as pirates, mercenaries, invaders and settlers.

Evidence from contemporary Egyptian sources and later biblical accounts concur with this image of wandering war-clans, armed for close-combat and extolling the virtues of the individual hero, imposing themselves on the peoples of Egypt and the Near East. There are also Greek and Latin accounts from late antiquity that cite a tradition of proto-Greek influence in the Nile delta, and of Egyptian and Asian influence on traditions beginning and probably antedating the Archaic period [700-500 B.C.] in Greece.

The peoples in question are many, and include refugees from Crete. We will focus primarily on two tribes that finally staked a claim in the lands of the Bible. The Dan were the tribe of Samson, known to the Greeks as the Danaean or Danoi, to the Egyptian scribes as the Danuna or Denyen, and to the biblical scribes as the Danites. The Dan were a small tribe of seafarers who were apparently kin to and rivals of the Philistines, and eventually ended their wanderings by merging with the tribes of Israel.

The Philistines are the people of Goliath, known to the Egyptian scribes as the Peleset, who gave their name to the land of Palestine. The Philistines appear to have been the largest tribe of the Sea Peoples who ravaged the Mediterranean. They are named as natives of Crete in two biblical passages [Jeremiah: 47, 4, Amos: 9, 7] served the Egyptians as mercenaries, invaded Egypt as part of a pirate confederacy looking for land to settle, and were apparently permitted by the Egyptian

Pharaoh –after a bloody draw in the Nile delta—to settle along the northern borders of the Egyptian Empire, occupying the coastal lands of the Bible as a kind of buffer force between Egypt and the Asian tribes. The Philistines were the bad guys in the *Book of Judges* and *Books of Samuel*.

It is during this period in the Old Testament of the Bible that an otherwise out-of-place attention to individual heroics appears in the scriptures. These are amplified in the works of Josepheus, complimented by later Greek traditions concerning Egypt, and have been partially confirmed by recent archaeology.

Map 6.
The Eastern Mediterranean –1225 to 950 B.C.
The principal locations cited in the author's study of the Sea Peoples.

"I slew the Denyen [who are] in their isles."
—Ramesses III

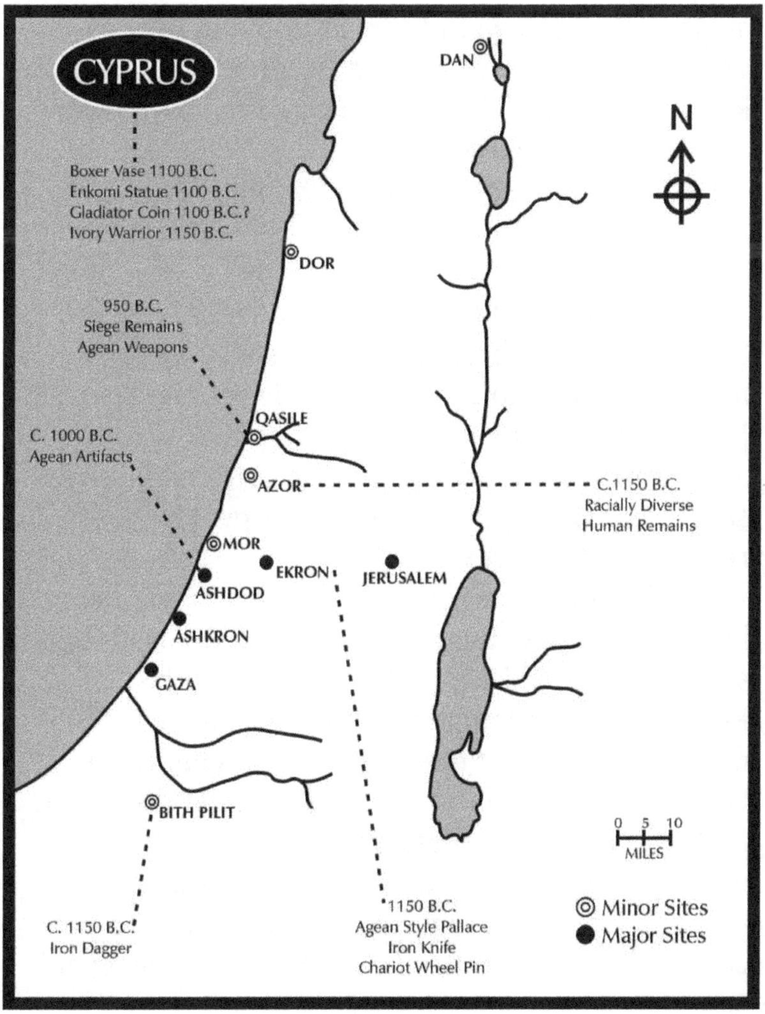

The Sea Peoples and the Spread of Heroic War Arts

"Benaiah son of Jehoiada, from Kabzeel, was a hero of many exploits. It was he who slew the two champions of Moab, and once went down into a pit and killed a lion on a snowy day. He also killed an Egyptian, a man of striking appearance armed with a spear. Benaiah went to meet him with a club, wrested the spear out of the Egyptian's hand, and killed him with his own weapon...David appointed him to his household."

—*Second Book of Samuel, 21, 22 and 23*

The biblical tale of Benaiah rings true. From the specific details concerning the slaying of the lion to the description of the duel with the Egyptian [which make it obvious that the "man of striking appearance" was fighting in Homeric fashion with shield and spear] the scriptures appear to be recalling actual events.

Not only does the story of Benaiah appear to be authentic, it is the closing act of heroics in that section of the Old Testament dealing with the Sea Peoples. This account curiously lays out all of the criteria required of the Greco-Roman heroes of classical and late antiquity, which are still extolled in 21st Century cinematic productions and videogames: the hero defeats multiple enemy heroes; defeats a dangerous beast in hand-to-paw combat; defeats a man of striking appearance; and is patronized by a powerful leader. Of course, the prototype of the ancient hero was Herakles, and it was believed by the ancients that the original Herakles was a resident of the Nile Delta –probably a feudal war-chieftain in the employ of Pharaoh whose men would have fought with shield and spear, and who was traditionally believed to have dueled with a club.

This was an age dominated by warlike individuals who personified the stark virtues described by Hesoid:

> "...men strange and powerful who loved
> the groans and violence of war!...
> Their hearts flinty hard,
> These were terrible men."

From the battlefields of Greece and Troy, to Crete, Rhodes, Cyprus, Palestine, Egypt, Sicily and Sardinia, the Sea People were the adventurers of their age, and their ethic of individual hand-to-hand combat had a profound effect on the military and athletic institutions of the western world. However, the area of their best recorded struggles in the Near East would soon be overrun by the supreme ancient ant-hill society of the Assyrians who waged pitiless wars of mass extermination, with the long term result that the lands of the Bible have since rarely produced a military culture capable of withstanding foreign incursions. The single exception seems to be the modern Israeli military which was heavily influenced by western military traditions.

This last point may seem a bit far a field in

the context of a book focused on prize-fighting. But, once one peers into the rich and controversial athletic histories of Greece and Rome, it will become apparent how important the warrior ethic of individual close-combat was to the very survival of these cultures both militarily and civically. It still has relevance to this day. During the quadruple high-jacking of American passenger jets on September 11, 2001, the only attack that failed was the one foiled by unarmed amateur athletes who were willing to engage in close combat.

On the Wine-dark Sea: A Warrior's View of Wrestling & Boxing c. 1000 B.C.

"But Zeus flung Strife on Akhaea's fast ships,
the brutal goddess flaring her storm-shield,
his terrible sign of war in both her fists."
-Homer, *The Iliad, from Agamemnon's Day of Glory*

Abider was not the embittered battle-scarred ship-takers that commanded most of the fleet's ships. The war-bosses had elected him as chief-of-supply simply because he was the only captain in this outfit that could speak to the Coast Dwellers well enough to barter, and the only one that could notate well enough to manage an inventory. All the same, he was a fighter and so were his men. And if he and his people were going to survive once they decided which Coast Dweller tribe deserved to lose their land, they better have their fight-legs under them when it came time for combat. Rowing was good for shield and spear strength.

But rowing wouldn't keep their minds sharp for combat or their body nimble enough for the type of skirmishing it was going to take to slaughter and subdue the stone-slinging goatherds his foraging parties would have to deal with on parallel marches once they got to decent country.

He had horse-breakers in his command from the high countries who loved to wrestle. For that he could spread hide piles on deck and have them go at it when the wind was right enough for the sail to do its work. Three of his boats were also crewed by dagger and shield fighters from Liar Island. Their training encompassed gauntlet fighting. Most of his people were spear-fighters who used no hand gear. But he could trim enough strips off of the wrestling hides so that every knucklehead on board his ships could hone their battle-sense with their fists and still have hands fit enough to man the oars when the wind died.

Shipboard competitions could lead to ship-to-ship contests when the fleet beached at night. Well, it could be easy to get carried away. But at least wrestling and fist-fighting would give all of these murderers and thieves something to do when they weren't burning villages.

Figure 21.
Cypriot Warrior
Bronze Statuette, Enkomi, Cyprus, c.1150 B.C.

This figure's round punching shield and overhand spear grip is echoed centuries later by the pottery illustrations of boxers in 6th Century B.C. Greece. This is a close combat stance readily generalized to a functional bare-knuckle boxing posture. Boxing would be a useful pastime for a warrior class which battled and dueled in this manner.

This figurine was apparently made by and for a society of metal workers. The indication for this deduction is the base of the figure, which is an ingot in the shape of an ox hide [the ancient smiths' symbol] which is not necessary for mounting as there is a fixture on the back of the figurine for fixing to a wall.

As an ancient fencing record this bronze statuette is indicative of the preferred dueling panoply of Danaian Samson; and the Philistine heroes... Benob whose bronze-tipped spear weighed 3.6 kilos; Goliath of Gath, who wielded a spear with a shaft equal to a weaver's beam with an iron head weighing 7.2 kilos [Goliath alone among the Biblical heroes also wielded a great sword]; the six-fingered Giant of Gath; and the Egyptian of striking appearance killed by Benaiah.

Military fencing with a thrusting spear and punching shield appears to be the war art from which archaic Greek boxing sprung, and there is some evidence that the Philistines and/or related tribes of sea peoples waylaying in Cyprus practiced a primitive form of boxing inherited from Minoan Crete.

Figure 22.
The Duelists
Sealstone, Late Minoan, Cyprus? c.1100 B.C.?

Though the origin of this item is vague* [and it may possibly belong among the material presented in the last chapter] it does solve the mystery of the short "rapiers" unearthed at various Minoan and Mykenain [proto-Greek] sites. Note the similarity in posture and artistic style to figure 23.

The aggressive use of the empty hand by these duelists suggests a weapon designed and used exclusively for the thrust. And, let us not forget that the thrust of the European dueling sword of the 17th Century laid the foundation for scientific boxing in England.

For a biblical commentary on the use of such blades let us look to 2nd Samuel 2:15-16… "So they came up, one by one, and took their places, twelve for Benjamin and Ishbosheth and twelve for David's men. Each man seized his opponent by the head and thrust his sword into his opponent's side; and thus they fell together."

In late antiquity when two evenly matched opponents dueled in the Roman arena with short cut-and–thrust swords without shields they were regarded as being engaged in a kind of mutual suicide. Indeed the Roman authorities employed such duels as a convenient means of dual execution. The head striking with the lead open hand demonstrated on this Philistine/Minoan sealstone suggests that the blades were not edged, or were two brittle for the beat, block or parry. Overall the illustration is most reminiscent of a modern American prison fight with shanks.

* Burn, A. R. Minoans, Philistines, and Greeks: B.C. 1400-900, Knopf, NY, 1930, page 160

Figure 23.
Cypriot Boxers
Mykenain krater [vase], under Minoan influence, Cyprus, c.1100 B.C.

This illustrates long range extended guard boxing of the type commonly practiced by converted fencers. The posture suggests the possibility of kicking, but it is more likely oriented toward a lunging thrust with the lead fist. It appears that the fighter on the left is the dominant boxer –keeping with the ancient Minoan tradition—and he appears to be stepping on right's foot.

From Samson to Herakles: The Cult of the Ultimate Loser

"And Samson, deeming it worse than all his misfortunes to be unable to avenge such insults, asked the boy who led him by the hand to lead him to the columns so he could rest. And when he was brought to the columns he flung his weight upon them, overturning the columns and bringing down the hall on the Lords of the Philistines, with whom he perished."

—Josephus, *Jewish Antiquities*

Courtesy of Joseph Bellofatto, for 2014 edition

The ages of the hero are three: (1) the age of the hero-god [Gilgamesh]; (2) the age of the traditional hero who serves as the bodyguard of the king such as Benaiah who commanded King David's select guard of mercenary Cherethites [Cretans] and Pelethites [Philistines]; and (3) the age of the heroic misfit such as Samson or Herakles who is strong enough to conquer but not wise enough to survive.

This last incarnation of the hero is the true prototype of the prize-fighting athlete. He is a man of the past symbolically struggling in the present through brutally proscribed rituals for the vicarious entertainment and education of a wider society, whose members, feel in their bones, that they have wandered too far from the ways of their distant ancestors, but have no way back to a simpler life, when a clan's very survival might hang on the actions of a single champion.

Society needs this champion to agonize, triumph, and finally go down in defeat. What it doesn't need is for this dynamic soul to actually belong. A society where this type of individual is an intricate functioning part of the whole is a society in crisis, and civilized people, with their many comforts and conventions, hope never to live in crisis. For this reason the prizefighter is drawn increasingly from the lower classes, those who live in a constant state of crisis in the substratum of civilization. In the time of Gilgamesh the prize-fighter was a king born to the gods. In the time of Akhilles he was the right hand of the king born to the wealthy. In the time of Socrates he was a symbol of his city's vigor born to the middle class; and by the time of Christ he was a prisoner-of-war or slave born to the doomed or to the lowest classes. And so he continues to be recruited from among the poor to this day, a heroic diversion to aid a vast collective memory, a fighter who is ultimately born to lose, so that the soft-bellied spectator may somehow feel that he has been spared that ultimate loss by way of not having contended for victory.

The classical hero was already a psychological bandage for an impotent society by the time of Samson, who died fighting the oppressors of a people who were not only afraid to fight for themselves, but afraid that he would fight in their stead and bring a test of courage on them—a test they must ultimately fail, because they were afraid more than anything, of being free. They would await their slavery to King David and his "prize-fighters" such as Benaiah, to finally know the complaisant serenity that Samson's doomed struggle had denied them. Most people who have lived since sell their souls in a similar fashion, souls that are occasionally aroused by the struggles of a prize-fighter, only to be put to rest by his ultimate failure to maintain the struggle.

This knowledge provides the key to understanding the controversial figure of the boxer, and his extreme cousins the duelist and MMA fighter. These men live on the edge of their potential as they fight on the edge of the social fabric that binds us.

Chapter 12
Bibliographical Guide

In order to put the specific reading into context I read as extensively as possible in religion, anthropology and prehistory. I must credit Barry Cunliffe's *The Extraordinary Voyage of Pytheas the Greek*, Walker & Co., NY, 2001, for inspiring me to look more deeply into the past.

Mallory, J.P. *In Search of the Indo-Europeans: Language, Archaeology and Myth*, Thames and Hudson, London, 1989, pages 7-272

This was the one work that served as an overall guide to the sources utilized in each chapter of. It is required reading for anyone interested in European origins.

Select Bibliography by Chapter

Chapter 6
Facing the Prime: The Origins of Boxing

O'Connell, Robert, L. *Of Arms and Men: A History of War, Weapons, and Aggression*, Oxford, NY, 1989, pages 2-30

O'Connell offers precious insight into the evolution and stagnation of military cultures. He is actually at his best when discussing WWI era naval operations.

Tannahill, Reay. *Flesh and Blood: A History of the Cannibal Complex*, Dorset, NY, 1975, pages 1-18

Read this while you are drunk and be sure to skip your next cookout!

Frazer, Sir James George. *The Golden Bough: A Study of Magic and Religion*, MacMillan, NY, 1922, pages 10-11, 96-125, 235-68, 305-40, 556-85, 669-85

To really absorb this and put it into a more modern context look up any number of works written or edited by Joseph Campbell. The easiest read is *The Power of Myth*.

Alexander, Michael. *Beowolf, A Verse Translation*, Penguin, 1973, NY, pages 9-49, 51-151

This crude epic is the most primal blood-drenched story-telling to survive the ages.

<u>Chapter 7</u>

Of Perfect Might: Ritual Combat in the Ancient Near East –2600 to 1000 B.C.

----. *Peoples and Places of the Past, The National Geographic Illustrated Cultural Atlas of the Ancient World*, Washington D.C., 1983, pages 22-116

The maps produced by The National Geographic Society are second to none in graphic quality and historical accuracy.

Shabandar, Sumya. *The Epic of Gilgamesh*, Garnet, Reading, Birkshire, 1994, pages 1-94

This is an unobtrusive translation of our oldest tale, of the big man and his ancestor who survived the flood. This story takes us back in time through an ancient mind's eye.

Bauman, Hans. *In The Land of Ur: The Discovery of Ancient Mesopotamia*, Pantheon, NY, 1969, pages 24-160

Much of the best material on the Near East was written in the 2nd and 3rd quarters of the 20th Century. This was a period of renewed access to the region and of passionate scholarship concerning biblical times.

Nemet-Nejat, Karen Rhea. *Daily Life in Ancient Mesopotamia*, Greenwood, Westport, CT, 1998, pages 11-334.

Most of the scholarship that focuses on the daily lives of ordinary people was written in the last quarter of the 20th Century. Previously the focus had been on the ruling classes.

Chapter 8

The Boxers of Egypt –2000 to 1151 B.C.

Shaw, Ian. General Editor. *The Oxford Illustrated History of Ancient Egypt*, Oxford, UK, 2000, pages 118-329

Baikie, James. *Egyptian Papyri and Papyrus Hunting*, the Religious Tract Society, London, 1925, pages 5-320

Bianchi, Robert Steven. *The Nubians: People of the Ancient Nile*, Milbrook, Brookfielt, CT, 1994, pages 38-54

Poliakoff, Michael B. Combat Sports in the Ancient World: Competition, Violence, and Culture, Yale, New Haven and London, 1987, 1-7, 64-67, 89-116,

Numerous secondary sources of a general nature, such as the National Geographic Atlas sited as a source for Chapter 1, above, were also accessed, primarily for the maps.

Chapter 9
When Boxers Were Kings: The Boxing Warriors of Crete –1700 to 1380 B.C.

Castleden, Rodeney. *Minoans: Life in Bronze Age Crete*, Routledge, London, 1990, pages ix-194
Of the 5 titles on ancient Crete accessed for this study, *Minoans*, was by far the superior source, with a wealth of sketches illustrating surviving artifacts, and a holistic treatment of the archaeological record utilized to illuminate the artifacts.

Chapter 10
On Hostile Shores: Prize-fighting from Samson to Goliath –1224 to 950 B.C.

The Old Testament, Revised English Bible & King James, *Judges, Samuel, Isaiah*

Josephus. *Jewish Antiquities,* Books IV-VI

Dothan, Trude & Moshe. *People of the Sea: The Search for the Philistines,* MacMillan, NY, 1992, pages 3-260

The authors shed light on their methods as well as their findings—indispensable.

Ancient Calendars

To better appreciate the life of the ancient prizefighter we should know something of his schedule and the cycles of important events that affected his career. Although the Babylonians and Egyptians abided by known calendars it is not evident that their ritual combats had any significant relationship to their measure of time. As for the Minoans, we don't know how they measured time and how –if any—their measure of time affected ritual combats. Based on the importance of sacred combat to the Greek and Roman calendars it might be assumed that earlier peoples also held ritual combats at specified times. For this reason the Babylonian calendar is provided opposite.

The Astronomers of Babylon

The scientist-priests of Babylon had a profound effect on Greek, Hebrew, Hellenistic and Roman measures of time. The Sabbath, the seven-day-week, the minute, the second, and the 24-hour day all originated in ancient Mesopotamia – birthplace of boxing so far as we know. Just for the record the Babylonian year started at the Vernal Equinox and constituted 12 lunar months:

1. *Nisan*
2. *Iyyar*
3. *Sivvan*
4. *Tammuz*
5. *Ab*
6. *Elul*
7. *Tisri*
8. *Marchesvan*
9. *Kislev*
10. *Tebet*
11. *Sebut*
12. *Adar*

The author is willing to go out on a limb and surmise that boxing and wrestling were Sabbath activities in Mesopotamia.

CPSIA information can be obtained
at www.ICGtesting.com
Printed in the USA
LVHW02s1804040618
579513LV00004B/1168/P

9 781505 384505